Twenty-Five Years of Slaying

Exploring the History and Cultural Impact of one of TV's greatest Cult Classics

Matthew L. Martin

Editor at Large, cultofwhatever.com

TWENTY-FIVE YEARS OF SLAYING

BY

MATTHEW
L. MARTIN

MATTHEW L. MARTIN

ISBN: 9798732202397

booksbymatthew.com

THE LATEST NOVELS,
SHORT STORIES,
AND POEMS,
AS WELL AS NEWS
ABOUT UPCOMING RELEASES.

ABOUT THE AUTHOR

Matthew Martin is a thirty-something husband and father of three. He is an avid reader, a part-time novelist, and an amateur poet. He has written online for various websites for the better part of a decade, having worked as a staff writer for The Sportster, TVOnline, and SB Nation.

He currently works as an editor-at-large for CultofWhatever.com, an entertainment site covering all manner of comic books, genre films, music, TV, pro wrestling, and just about anything (and everything) else in the world of cult entertainment.

He first watched Buffy the Vampire Slayer on a black and white 13-inch TV on the day it aired on the WB Network. He remembers liking it, attempting to talk to schoolmates about it, discovering he was alone in his love, and quietly watching it every week (twice a week once Angel debuted) with no one to talk to about it.

The internet has been great.

MATTHEW L. MARTIN

TABLE OF CONTENTS

BUFFY THE VAMPIRE SLAYER

INTRODUCTION

Debuting on March 10, 1997, Buffy the Vampire Slayer came to the WB Network as a mid-season replacement show. Based on the 1992 film of the same name, this show was overseen entirely by Joss Whedon, who wrote the screenplay for the film but was horrified to see how butchered his work was in the final product.

As the showrunner for the TV show, Whedon was able to tell long-form stories, develop characters slowly, and experiment with different styles and filmmaking techniques that couldn't be done in a single, two-hour format. Because of his willingness to experiment and his abject refusal to be traditional and "usual" with his show, Buffy the Vampire Slayer became—over the course of its seven-year run—one of the most groundbreaking, influential, and unpredictable shows in television history.

The show was made in the years before the revolution of modern television. These were the years before Mad Men, Breaking Bad, and The Wire brought a level of drama and acting previously unseen on television. This was before Game of Thrones and The Mandalorian brought feature film budgets and special effects out of the theaters and into the home.

Buffy the Vampire Slayer was not a Netflix original. It wasn't an HBO showcase. It wasn't made with a big budget and, despite its loyal fan following, it existed for almost its entire run living season to season, with the threat of cancelation always lingering, unsure if its current run of episodes would be the show's last.

With such technical and production restrictions in place, Whedon and his team of writers allowed their creativity to thrive, and even though some of the seams are showing in the audio/video quality, the heart is still there and, as the show hits its twenty-fifth anniversary, the quality of the writing is still evident, as is the passion poured into the characters by its tremendous cast.

MATTHEW L. MARTIN

If Buffy isn't a show you've seen before, if you never could get past the (intentionally silly) name, or if you're a long-time fan who, like me, grew up with the likes of Buffy, Xander, Willow, Giles, Cordy, Angel and the rest, then consider this your ultimate (spoiler-filled) look-back on one of the true gems of late-20th century television.

Chapter One

BUFFY SEASON ONE

Buffy's first season is easily the show's weakest entry, and yet, despite its many shortcomings and misfires, there are enough flakes of gold to be found to make a viewer continue digging for the real nuggets of greatness that will be enjoyed in the years to come.

Only two of the season's twelve episodes are rated highly (by me), with the third-best outing placing about halfway through the countdown. Nevertheless, with those two standouts, the show realized what it can be and what makes it so special, and uses those two as the templates to follow for the six seasons that came after.

Usually, a show's creative team takes in feedback from fans as a season is ongoing. Ratings reflect what storylines and character ideas are working, and which need revamping (or dropping entirely). Online responses provide the harshest and most unapologetically raw commentary possible on the quality of a character, an episode, or a season-long arc.

Starting with Buffy's second season, Joss Whedon and his writing staff would use the still-burgeoning internet to get instant, real-time feedback on the direction of each season, and unlike some creative types, Whedon listened to the fans and, even when he disagreed with their desires for some things and loathing of others, he almost always, in his own way, accommodated the wants and wishes of the masses. I say "in his own way" because, as fans of both Buffy and Angel can attest, Joss Whedon has a way of giving you what you want only long enough for you to love it...just so he can yank it brutally and tearfully away from you.

If there's one constant through the eight years of Buffy and Angel, it's that Joss Whedon is a glutton for your punishment.

But while Buffy's writer's room employed the feedback from the viewers from season two onward, they did not have that luxury during season one. That's because the entirety of Buffy's debut year was written, filmed, and edited for release all before a single second of footage aired on The WB.

The show launched as a replacement series after the primetime soap opera Savannah (midway through its second season) failed to find an audience and was canceled in late-1996. Its final episodes were produced and aired in January and February of 1997, leaving the final three months of WB's Network TV season without any content to air.

Typically a Network would just release syndicated shows or reruns to fill the final three months of first-run airtime, but with The WB being a young and fledgling network it was actually a cheaper alternative to put a new show on the air to fill the space. The only catch was everything would need to be produced ahead of time, to ensure the Network would have enough content to last until late-May/early-June.

Thus, Buffy the Vampire Slayer—a show with a silly name, a relatively unknown cast, a hokey "horror movie-meets-high school drama" backdrop, an unproved TV creative team, and on a little-watched network—dropped twelve episodes in as many weeks, produced with only the unshakeable confidence in its head-writer/creator to vouch for it. Everyone working on the show believed it would be a one-and-done series never to see a second year. Series star Sarah Michelle Geller was told not to worry about working on the show, as she was "sure to find real work next year."

Instead, rocky though it was, Buffy's first season was a success, enough for The WB to greenlight a second season after the first one ended to great reviews.

The central premise behind Buffy is established in the opening scene of the first episode: A pair of high schoolers—a suspicious-looking jock and his nervous blonde lady friend—sneak around the hallway of their school at night. It's a scene seen in many a horror movie. We know where this is going: The blonde is done for. Except no, after checking that the coast is clear, the blonde bares her vampiric teeth and sinks her fangs into her date, making him into a meal and making the audience watching at home into surprised (but satisfied) viewers.

The idea of subverting expectations—specifically with regard to gender—is at the crux of Buffy's mission statement. Whedon said that he wanted to turn the cliched notion of "the ditzy blonde being the damsel in distress" on its head, to make her into the hero and "the thing that monsters have nightmares about." The other overarching theme of the first season (which only evolved and grew as the characters did) was the phrase "high school is hell." It's a line uttered by anyone old enough to have survived high school, but in Buffy's world it's taken literally. The personal demons an adolescent faces are presented in the show as actual demons, and while the metaphors sometimes landed a bit awkwardly and heavy-handedly in season one, the writers would continue to fine-tune things in years to come, developing a better balance between the horror, drama, and comedy that would come to define the show's identity.

Most importantly, Joss and his writers never forced themselves to continue doing something just because it was "always done that way." Buffy's creative team frequently shook up the status quo, never letting things get too comfortable, too predictable, or—worst of all—too boring. Characters that, in lesser shows, would stick around as background players and bit parts for the duration of the series might, on Buffy, grow and evolve into major players, or they might die in shocking ways.

Other characters that, in lesser shows, would wear "plot armor" that protected them from mortal danger might, on Buffy, find themselves also dying in shocking ways. No one is safe in the world of Buffy and Angel but it's a testament to the writers and actors that almost every major character who dies in these two series (and there are a lot of them) are characters whose deaths create a powerful, visceral reaction out of the audience. There are no cheap deaths. There are no unearned deaths. And there are no consequence-free deaths.

When things happen on Buffy, they last.

That sense of unpredictability is best seen in the show's various season finale episodes. Because Buffy was always on the brink of cancellation, Whedon never knew if the finale he was writing would be the end of the "season" or the end of the whole "series." As such, he always wrote the final episode of the season to work, not only as the end of the storyline/arc being told that year, but also as the wrap-up to the whole show itself.

The only exception to this was in season six (coincidentally, it's the only season finale not directly credited to Joss Whedon) which was the first for Buffy to air on UPN. The show switched networks after its fifth season and was picked up with a guaranteed two-year deal, meaning season six was the first to be made with the understanding that a follow-up was going to happen. Not surprisingly, it's the only true cliffhanger of the seven finales. The others all end with a strong note of finality (season four's ending is a bit more complicated, with a season finale-like episode coming one week early, followed by an episode-long coda, but more on that when we get to it).

Buffy's first season is a rocky one, with monsters and plots that are cheap, dated, and unrefined in all the worst ways, but every episode has at least one hilarious moment, at least one clever scene, and at least one interesting idea, and, as said, the two episodes that stand out the best—episode 7's "Angel" and the season finale's "Prophesy Girl"—provide the show with the template Joss and co. would use to build its entire identity around.

In "Angel," Buffy discovers that the young man of mystery that's been popping in to aid her in her work as the Slayer (and whom she's been falling for) is actually a vampire himself. "Angel" is the first episode of the show that eschews the "freak of the week" format and instead lets the characters and "lore" of the show carry the drama. It works, and because it works, the writers walked into season two with the confidence that they could tell more stories that were about their characters, without having to rely solely on a gimmick-monster driving the plot.

In the case of season one, the year ends with Buffy wrestling with and overcoming the question at the heart of the arc for the season: Does she still want to be the Slayer? When confronted with her destiny in the first episode of the series, her instinct is to run from it. By the end, she is marching confidently toward the final battle while her theme music plays.

Prophesy Girl is the first episode Joss Whedon directed and he would go on to be the show's greatest asset behind the camera. His talents as a writer were already well-established (Toy Story, for one) but it was on Buffy where he grew into the director that would eventually helm the first two Avengers movies. He even said that he used the show as on-the-job training for becoming a feature film director, and the episodes with his name attached as director are almost always experimental, epic, or significant in one way or another.

Every Buffy season explores a key aspect of life and maturity befitting the title character's age and development. In season one, Buffy tackles her calling. In season two, it's her first love. In season three, it's the end of childhood.

In season four, it's the awkward transition between being immature and mature. In season five, it's the grim realities of adulthood. Season six is more introspective as the true villains of the season are the three heroes themselves; the theme is the messiness of living without parents or guardians shepherding you.

MATTHEW L. MARTIN

The final season is about letting go and moving into adulthood for good. These themes are introspective by nature but they're explored in Buffy's world through monsters, magic, and mayhem of both the horrific and hilarious kinds.

There simply is no other show like it.

Buffy is a show about kids becoming adults and dealing with the challenges of letting go of youth. Incidentally, its sister-show Angel is about newly-christened adults dealing with the challenges of adulthood.

Angel tackles the grown-up struggles of managing a start-up company and dealing with staff turnover and legal troubles (season one), with finding its footing as a functional company, while dealing with personal problems messing with the workplace (season two), with growing and expanding the operation with new staff, while ostracizing a once pivotal partner (season three), with the challenges that come with trying to get over the hump, while family drama pushes against workplace responsibilities (season four), and finally with selling out to the man and suffering the feeling of hypocrisy that follows (season five).

Angel starts from the sort of emotional place where Buffy's seventh season ends. Angel's show is not about growing into adulthood; it's about living with it. They're two very different shows, despite sharing so much of the same DNA, and are equally excellent for different reasons.

Chapter Two

BUFFY SEASON TWO

Buffy's first season was a rocky one, being that it was entirely written, filmed, and edited for release before a single episode ever made it to airwaves. Showrunner Joss Whedon and his staff of writers (skilled in genres of comedy, drama, or science-fiction), were unable to hear any criticism or encouragement regarding any of the show's initial strengths and weaknesses.

Still, there was an obvious confidence in the material and the finale was excellent: The WB greenlit a sequel season soon after the first one ended. The twenty-two episodes that followed would comprise a season that turned Buffy the Vampire Slayer from a "quirky and fun little genre show," into the future "cult favorite" it remains today.

Buffy's second season is a tale of two halves, the first half being the show it was and the second being the show it would become.

The first ten episodes of season two feel like a better put-together continuation of the first season, with the same "freak of the week" plot structure, and reliance on "hokey but charming" situational drama, comedy, and horror, depending on the moment (and sometimes all three in the same scene).

It would be easy to dismiss the first half, with lower-tier episodes like "Inka Mummy Girl" (which sees the gang contend with...an Inka mummy girl) and "Some Assembly Required" (where Buffy has to stop a kind of Frankenstein's monster/resurrected star football player), and think the show had found a low-stakes groove and was primed to settle into a few years on the air being little more than TV fluff.

That's not what happened, however, and there are three key things elevating the opening of season two, which are done well enough as to make a viewer on the fence stick with the show in time to see it take its massive leap forward in quality.

MATTHEW L. MARTIN

The first comes in the second episode, which sees the debut of this season's big bad: Spike. If you're not familiar with what will become the template for Buffy, there are basically three things happening in any given episode: The first is the forty-five-minute plot driving that week's action. The second involves some use of the season-long external threat that is looming over everything (the so-called "big bad" of the year). Finally, there's the introspective angle that Buffy is wrestling with in any given season.

In season one, a typical Buffy episode would see the heroine contend with a killer robot, for example. At the same time, we're reminded either through an action scene, a cutaway, or a bit of dialogue, that the villain's big bad for the season (in season one it was the Nosferatu-looking monster, The Master) is plotting and scheming like Rita Repulsa on the moon. Also at the same time, Buffy would be fighting her inward challenge which, in season one, was her reluctance to embrace the mantel of Vampire Slayer.

Every year brings Buffy a new "big bad" to contend with and a new personal challenge to overcome. Since the show is, ultimately, one big metaphor for growing up, those personal challenges tend to relate to that journey: In season two, Buffy has to contend with the personal struggles that come with having a first serious love interest, the vampire with a soul, Angel. At the same time, there's a new big bad in town, who just so happens to have a lot of history with that love interest.

Unlike The Master—who looked like he stepped out of a silent movie horror show, with his drab clothing, monstrous face, and Max Schreck-looking fangs—Spike is a Vampire for the late-20th century. He wears a leather duster jacket, has bleached-blond hair, swaggers when he walks, and talks with the confidence of a Vamp that's killed not one but two slayers in his long life of evil. His first episode sees him monologue about eating a hippy at Woodstock and spending the next few hours watching his hand move in front of his face, before he snaps and murders the villain we were led to believe would be the season's big bad.

Spike was a revelation. He's the kind of instantly-captivating character that electrifies a scene and makes the already confident show feel like it had always been missing something before he arrived.

The second step forward in quality for the first half of the season comes with a pair of episodes that aired back-to-back, "Halloween" and "Lie to Me." The former is easily the best romp-episode of the show thus far, getting every ounce of comedic value out of every character in the cast (something the show would do simply effortlessly as it progressed), while the latter is a darker, more character-focused outing.

To this point in the show, very few episodes had eschewed the "freak of the week" plot device. A Buffy episode almost always had some kind of one-off bad guy to be dealt with. In this case, the one-off baddie isn't a monster or a demon; it's an old friend of Buffy's who just wants to become a vampire so he can avoid the death sentence his cancer has brought him. It's the first episode since the season one finale that puts the heart of the drama not on a fight with a monster but on a character making tough choices, and the success of the episode gave Whedon and co. the confidence to produce more hour-long outings that were about "people who happen to contend with monsters," and fewer about "people fighting monsters."

The final big step forward in the first half of the season was the two-part episode "What's My Line" which, in retrospect, was sort of a mini-season finale, wrapping up a lot of the Spike vs Buffy plot that had been bubbling since episode two. Soon after this, the season (and the series) would take a turn like no other, and Spike's role as primary antagonist would never be the same. In that case he and his love Drusilla (played exceptionally by Juliet Landau) make the most of their last big hurrah as big(gest) bads, even though it wasn't yet apparent that they were about to be usurped.

Throughout the first half of season two, despite many of the episodes feeling like holdovers from season one, there was a strong throughline of Buffy and Angel's blossoming relationship elevating everything else around it. The progression of their story this year made some kind of a climax inevitable. That climax came in the two-part mid-season showcase: "Surprise" and "Innocence," which took the real-world horror of "girl sleeps with boy and wakes up to find he has changed" and put it within the context of a world full of vampires, magic, and demons with and without conscience-possessing souls.

Angel is a vampire "cursed" with a soul. That word is critical to understanding his character; he's not blessed. It wasn't a gift. He was once a ruthless barbarian demon, one of (if not the) most feared of his kind ever to roam the earth. But when he crossed the wrong people and tortured a group of Romani ("gypsies" as the show calls them), they cursed him in the most creative way possible:

By restoring Angel's soul but maintaining his vampirism, Angel was forced to feel the guilt of centuries of horror he inflicted. He spent the next several generations in isolation, living off rats, too guilt-ridden to feast on people, and never found a purpose in life until he met Buffy and decided to help her fight those who are as evil as he used to be.

But the Romanis curse carried a catch.

Should Angel ever feel absolute, contented bliss, a "moment of pure happiness," his soul would be taken from him and he would return to his barbaric, cruel, former self, the Vampire Angelus. That moment of bliss came after sleeping with Buffy. It wasn't the sex that changed him back to Angelus (that's a common misconception even among characters in the two shows), but rather it was the peaceful and quiet moments that followed. With contentment achieved, the Romani curse twisted its knife, and Angel was no more.

The remainder of season two follows Buffy as she wrestles with what happened to her lover. She moves between feelings of shame over causing Angelus' return, to guilt over the same, to depression over losing him, to fierce determination that she can save him until, finally, the grim realization that she has to kill him.

As wonderful as Spike was as a bad guy you loved to watch, Angelus was an absolute scene/season stealer. His first moment features him taking a bite out of a lady who just inhaled a cigarette, and even though there's no biological way it should happen, when Angel unlatches his fangs from her neck, he exhales the vapor as if he'd just taken a drag himself...

It's a moment that makes no "sense," but is all about "style." It's about setting a mood and establishing how different Angelus is compared to Angel. In this one scene, Joss Whedon instantly told us exactly who this new version of Angel is.

"Innocence" is a Whedon-directed episode, only his fourth of the series so far, and already he shows a carefree "just go for it" attitude, unconcerned about the stodgy old rules of TV making or the way things "ought to be." No hyperbole: Joss is the TV director's Steven Spielberg; he just had a knack for creating scene after scene with memorable moments that transcended the medium itself.

There are still a few one-off episodes that followed "Surprise" and "Innocence," like "Killed by Death" or the underrated "Bewitched, Bothered, and Bewildered," but the quality of the writing was stronger across the board, the pacing was snappier, and everything felt a little more supercharged in the wake of the two pivotal episodes mid-season.

This was the true turning point of the show and even though there would be stronger seasons overall still to come, when examining the whole seven-year series, there's a very clear divide that all fans can agree on: There's the show before "Surprise/Innocence" and there's the show after it.

The real brilliance of the Angelus arc is that it was an arc at all. Had it been the kind of one-episode problem to solve that so many episodes had done before, it would have gone down as a fun twist, quickly forgotten. Instead, Angelus remained evil, week after week, episode after episode, and just to ensure you sympathized with Xander's almost eager readiness to stake the vamp's heart and be done with him, Joss and co. made sure Angelus did some horrific and potentially unforgivable things. The climax of that came in the episode "Passion," one of the show's very best and the moment when everyone knew: Angelus has to be killed.

The story of Buffy and Angel is almost Shakespearean, had the thespian ever dipped his toes in the waters of horror-fantasy. Joss himself is a literal student of Shakespeare, having studied the playwright at Winchester College in England.

The Shakespearean approach to the Buffy/Angel dynamic was woven throughout the multi-episode arc, but was never more overtly commented on by the show than in the episode "I Only Have Eyes for You." The criminally underrated episode features the ghosts of dead lovers (tragic, ill-fated lovers, of course) possessing students and forcing them to reenact their final moments of life. The episode comes to a head when Buffy and Angelus are possessed by the lovers, forget who they are, and wax poetic about the nature of their doomed love. It's a powerfully acted and wonderfully written scene that's almost meta in the way it comments on the Angel/Buffy relationship and how it has been undone by the return of Angelus.

After that, and the embarrassingly out of place "freak of the week" episode "Go Fish," all that is left is the two-part finale of the season, which features Angelus on a quest to unleash a demon on the world that would destroy... everything, forcing Spike to turn against him because, in his words "I like people, bunch of little Happy Meals with legs," while the rest of the gang work on a counter-spell that will restore Angelus' soul.

There are so many seeds planted in this episode that will sprout and bear fruit in seasons (and shows) to come, from Willow showing her proficiency in working magic, to Spike's first taste of working for the good guys, to the tragedy of Angel and Buffy's broken relationship coming to a head.

In the episode's final moments, three important things happen in very quick succession, but it's the order in which they happen that make it the most Shakespearean, dramatic, and gut-wrenching finale of the show: Angelus unleashes the world-ending demon (that can only be stopped with the death of the one who unleashed him), Willow restores Angelus' soul, and Buffy drives her sword through Angel's heart, sending him into whatever hell dimension the demon was about to ascend from.

That Buffy does what she does after Angel is restored is what makes the episode so special: A copout finish would have been for Willow's spell to work either too late or early enough to happen before the demon was unleashed. Instead, Angelus accomplishes his mission, meaning his death had to happen. From there, the cheap finish would have been for Buffy to stab Angelus and then restore his soul, but that would take the choice out of Buffy's hands, and if there's one thing this show loves to do, it's give its characters hard choices to make and then force them to live with the consequences of those choices.

Buffy sees Angel return to her, then she tells him to close her eyes, and then she runs him through. Drama like that is earned, and the show will make Buffy live with the consequences of her actions for a long time to come.

Season two might have had a few of the same "meh" episodes that hindered season one, but once it found its stride, it became destination television for its legion of fans. Small, incremental steps forward happen throughout the first half of the season before the show takes a massive jump in quality that will continue for the remainder of its run.

Buffy's first year was all about coping with her calling as the Slayer. Season two is about the challenges that come with a very complicated first love. Next season brings Buffy to her senior year of High School. As you can imagine, there's much drama to mine from that setting, and with it, the show will have its most consistently great year of them all...

Chapter Three

BUFFY SEASON THREE

After two seasons on the air, it had already become apparent that Joss Whedon and co. had a handle on how to present the core ideas behind the stories of Buffy and the Scooby Gang.

And what are those core ideas? For one, it's the notion of taking the teenage mantra "high school is hell" and making it literal: Instead of fighting proverbial demons, in the Buffyverse teens must contend with actual demons, while still struggling with all the "usual" drama that comes with being in High School. That drama is almost always filtered through the prism of this fantastical world and seen through the eyes of the heroine in the center, as she grows from teenager to adult.

As we've noticed before, each of Buffy's seven seasons tackles some part of the maturation process, whether it's accepting who you are (season one) or dealing with a first love (season two). Except who is Buffy? She's not just an adolescent grappling with teenage drama; she's the Slayer, a veritable superhero with the weight (and the fate) of the world on her shoulders, knowing not only that she has countless vampires, demons, and other monsters all vying to be the one to kill her, but also knowing that when she does die, her powers will simply transfer to the next "chosen" girl, who will carry on the fight after her.

In a twisted way, the very thing that makes Buffy so special and unique (she is the one Slayer) is also what makes her just one in a very long line of girls. She's not the first Slayer; she's more like the one-hundred thousandth Slayer, knowing full well that she will one day die and all she accomplished—all her many feats, all the victories she won that impressed and spellbound so many—will just move to the next one to pick up right where she left off as if she never existed. If you don't think that's worthy of an existential crisis, you're crazy. That's the underpinning that drives Buffy's first season.

The trouble with season one was it didn't quite live up to that lofty premise and instead "settled" for run-of-the-mill "freak of the week" plot devices and a very episodic television format. Some of that is because this particular era of network television necessitated weekly plots and an episodic delivery. Some of it was because the show was still trying to figure itself out. Either way, Buffy's first year can best be described as having "unrealized promise."

Season two was a dramatic leap forward.

Once again, the show took the real-world struggle—in this case "a girl's first serious romance"—and wove it elegantly throughout the supernatural-filled season. Buffy's second year is cleanly split into two halves, with the first being everything leading up to the epic two-parter "Surprise/Innocence," and the second dealing with the fallout. In the build-up episodes, the Buffy/Angel romance is a budding one, flirting with the overused will-they/won't-they trope, walking the viewer right to the edge of the cliff before savagely pushing us off at the end of "Surprise."

Angel's turn to evil allows the writers to keep things from getting stale, adds a new villainous wrinkle to an already loaded cast of baddies (Spike and Drusilla, plus a host of one-off monsters), and creates a wellspring of drama in a plethora of ways (Buffy's personal struggles, the death of Mrs. Calendar, the constant fear that Angelus might pop in, if only for a quick "boo!"), all in one fell swoop. It was a masterstroke of an idea, executed perfectly, and climaxed with (in my opinion) the series' very best finale.

All of the emotion, the drama, the anger, the suspense, and the excitement peaked exactly when it should, right in time for the final few minutes of the second season. If there were any doubts that Buffy deserved a third year, "Becoming 1-2" drove a sword right through them and kicked them backward into a hell dimension.

If there is a flaw in season two, it's that the overall arc of Buffy dealing with her first love was, at times, played a bit too subtly, to the point where a viewer might not even realize what the allegory of the season was until Angelus appeared in "Innocence." It was something for the next season to improve upon, and boy did it...

Buffy's third season is the series' best.

Maybe the thing I love the most about it—and that's a very long list—is that it's the season where the show finally clicked in every conceivable way. The humor had never been better, the drama was pitch-perfect, the supernatural thrills (the show was rarely ever genuinely scary) were all excellently balanced with the day-to-day "normal" drama, while the driving arc of the season looms over everything like a bomb slowly ticking down to zero. This was the year where everything Joss and co. learned in seasons one and two were put into practice, so naturally this is the year where they ended things by blowing up half of the show and resetting the table for season four.

Season three is Buffy's senior year in high school, and there is no greater source of drama from which to mine than teenagers faced with the reality that, whether they are mature enough or not (and most are not), Graduation Day is looming and when it arrives it will spit them all out into the real world one way or another. Unlike in season two, which only halfway touched on its year-long theme in the first half of the season, Buffy's third year is saturated with talk about graduation, wrestling with the angst that comes with graduation, feeling the pressure over being unprepared for graduation, and so on.

Creating a supernatural foil to contend with is Sunnydale's enigmatic Mayor, previously only alluded to and now given a spotlight role as the big bad of the season. Mayor Wilkins is a man who wants to become a demon and he has pegged Sunnydale High's graduation day as his "ascension" day, when he will transform into a huge, snake-like monster and devour the whole student body as his first demonic meal.

Complicating things is Faith, the new Slayer in town. She is the replacement for Kendra (barely mentioned in the season two write-up because, well, look how quickly she was brushed aside to make way for Faith) who, herself, was the replacement for Buffy (who was dead for a minute at the end of season one).

The rule that there can be only one Slayer is still technically true, and despite what I said earlier, to be technical: Faith is the Slayer but Buffy—by virtue of being resuscitated—still retains all the Slayer's powers and—by virtue of her character development in season one—retains the inner feeling of destiny and purpose that compels her to keep fighting the fight.

So where does that leave Faith? She's in limbo, detached from the Scooby gang and forced to make her own rules (which get her into trouble and drive her away, right into the arms of the evil Mayor).

Faith is a phenomenal addition to the cast.

In many ways she represents the path Buffy could have gone down had she not had the support system around her that we've come to love over the past two years: Willow, Giles, and

Xander are Buffy's heart, mind, and spirit; her mother provides a stable home, Angel (back from his hell dimension) is a complication but still is a support in more ways than one.

Faith, on the other hand, grew up with the worst of circumstances. She had an unloving home, no friends, no guardians or mentors to give her encouragement, no "love" life of any kind. In short, Buffy being the Slayer is a constant burden, because it always clashes with her own (deeply rooted, but still selfish) desires to be "just a normal girl." Faith, on the other hand, sees being the Slayer as her identity, a purpose she has always sought after.

Buffy didn't need to be the Slayer to feel complete; it was something added to her that she spends seven years coming to terms with. Faith needs to be the Slayer the power of the Slayer, or at least she thinks she does; it's what she thinks makes her life have meaning. Because of that, and despite her very tough outer shell, she's really the most vulnerable and fragile character of them all, making her the perfect person to be seduced by the darkside in the now-expected midseason twist.

With Faith on his side, the Mayor looks unstoppable, and as the Scooby Gang deals with how to stop Wilkins from unleashing a fully-formed demon, they also contend with ending the biggest chapter of their lives. Much of season three is therefore about coming to terms with self, something that is healthy and important as a teen prepares to graduate.

Xander and Willow strike up an illicit relationship this year, after they both find the perfect partner in Cordelia and Oz. Why do they do it? Because impending graduation makes teens do some of their first serious reflection and navel-gazing about their lives thus far. It's something that happens again when you turn thirty, again when you turn forty, again when you turn fifty, then it takes a break until you turn sixty-five. At that point, you pretty much spend the rest of your life bouncing back and forth between navel-gazing and enjoying retirement.

So you can forgive a high school senior for the existential crisis that comes as the final day of "childhood dependence" ends and the transition to "adult independence" begins.

Buffy goes through a similar crisis of identity, as she secretly craves the freedom that Faith lives by so cavalierly. Angel—not graduating but caught up in it—goes through it too, as he starts to feel he can do more good outside of Sunnydale. Giles also winces at the prospect of not being the indispensable brains of the team anymore; a bunch of college kids won't exactly be hanging around at the school library next year.

MATTHEW L. MARTIN

So how does the show tackle these crises of identity? With episodes like "The Zeppo" (Xander flies solo while the rest of the gang save the world), "The Wish" (Cordy deals with an alternate universe where Buffy was never around to screw up her life), "Lovers Walk" (Xander and Willow's affair catches up to them), "Dopplegangland" (Willow looks darkly into the reflection of her 'mirror universe' self), and "Helpless" (Buffy loses her powers and her trust in Giles).

Episode after episode, in this nearly flawless season, focuses in one way or another on the big themes at work this year. It makes season three (along with season five) feel like a modern, serialized TV show, despite most episodes being self-contained.

And as the year draws to a close it does such a spectacular job tying together those themes and bringing everything to such a satisfying conclusion that the whole series could have ended with Graduation Day 1-2 and the show still would have been regarded as one of the best ever. And the episode that perfectly nails the feeling of thematic closure is the penultimate of the season (if we consider the two-part finale as a single unit), "The Prom."

To this point in the show, Buffy (the character) operated as a kind of Spider-Man;

doing good on a local level and balancing super-heroics with a secret identity. Over the course of the first three seasons, though, her good deeds started to pile up in the form of background players, bit parts, and ancillary characters that she helped along the way. No one better represented that segment of the extended cast than the loveable sad sack Jonathan.

Going all the way back to the early episodes of the show, Jonathan was a go-to character if ever there needed to be someone to represent the nerds, the dweebs, and the kinds of losers that today rule the world but in the 90s were the biggest target for high school bullies.

Jonathan was the center of one of Buffy's more controversial episodes, Earshot, which dealt with the school shooting epidemic that plagued campuses across the country for a twenty-year stretch. This being Buffy, there had to be a supernatural twist; in this case, Buffy has a run-in with a demon whose blood infects her, causing her to develop the ability to hear the thoughts of the people around her.

Much hilarity ensues until Buffy overhears one student seemingly plotting to open fire on his classmates. In the end, it ended up being a misunderstanding (it was actually the lunch lady planning on poisoning the students), but still Buffy finds Jonathan with a loaded rifle...about to take his own life. She talks him down and the episode ends on a high note...but that didn't stop the network from refusing to air it until weeks before the season four premiere. To be fair, the Columbine Shooting had occurred just one week prior, so everyone was a little sensitive. Personally, I think the message of the episode would have been helpful, not hurtful, had it aired as scheduled.

Jonathan being saved by Buffy paid off in a big way in "The Prom," in which the perpetually overlooked, side-eyed, and misunderstood school girl is formally recognized by her peers. Jonathan makes a speech saying what everyone in the school thinks but dares not to say: They're ground zero for freaky stuff, monster attacks, and more, and more than twice Buffy Summers has been in the thick of it, keeping them safe. With that, he bestows upon her the "Class Protector" award and creates one of the sweetest and "earned" feel-good moments I've ever seen on TV.

It's the perfect way to end the episode before the finale, which features in its climax the entire school banding together to stop the Mayor's ascension. The climactic fight of the season maybe isn't as visceral and budget-busting as Joss would do in The Avengers, but for a TV show (with a shoestring budget) it works, and it mostly works because the director made it about the characters. If you don't care about the people in the fight then special effects can only take you so far. If you do care, no special effects are needed at all.

Buffy's third season built beautifully to a conclusion three years in the making and, at the end of it, the show had boldly declared that the next year (if there would be a next year) would have to shake up the formula in order to proceed. As you probably know, there would indeed be a fourth season greenlit by the WB Network and, true to his word, Joss offered up the Buffy we knew with more than a few new wrinkles to play around with...and a brand new show—Angel—to compliment things.

Chapter Four

ANGEL SEASON ONE

Similar to Buffy, Angel needed about a dozen episodes under his belt before he started to find his groove. Nevertheless, the noir-laden aesthetic that would define the series was present from the very beginning.

The spinoff never quite reached the level of influence in the cultural zeitgeist as did Buffy but it has its fans, many of whom regard it as the superior show. For a science-fiction comparison, Buffy is to Star Trek: The Next Generation what Angel is to Star Trek: Deep Space Nine. It was darker, slower-paced, more serialized, and more devoted to developing a core cast of characters.

Probably the biggest difference between the two shows was the willingness of Angel to experiment with its major themes and structure. Buffy basically had a formula that was defined for her show as early as season two, and the series hardly deviated from it until, arguably, the end of the final season.

For the most part, Buffy had a theme to explore in each season, both internal and external, and a big bad that challenged her as she explored that theme. Angel, on the other hand, never sat still or kept true to a single formula. Instead of a season-long big bad that changed every year, Angel had one that overshadowed the whole series, as well as two or sometimes three lesser big bads to contend with every season...until the fifth when they had none.

Instead of one season-long arc that took the characters on a journey, Angel relied on multiple mini-arcs...except for the third where they had just one. Instead of both an internal and an external goal to achieve, Angel blurred the lines between the two, taking its lead character on much more of a developing journey than Buffy ever had, except for the first where he was mostly static.

Do you see what I mean? Angel often went out of its way not to do things the way they were done on Buffy, but the showrunners also never let the show find a groove and ride it to the end. Things were always shifting around. That might be because the WB Network never seemed happy with the ratings or the tone of the show, and were always pressuring Joss and co. to shake things up, but it could also be that, because it was the spinoff, the B-show, the other Buffyverse series, the creators knew they had more of a license to play around and try new things.

During the show's time on air, Joss remarked that Angel was the only show on the WB Network that wasn't trying to be like Buffy, and that was clearly a deliberate choice, as evidenced by the show's first season. There's no easy way to rate the five years Angel was on the air, season by season, nor are there near as many stand-out episodes to point to (though there are a few).

The show is better considered in chunks; half a season here, a third of a season there, a few two or three parters, etc. Some of these mini-arcs are among the best Buffyverse content you'll find anywhere. Some are flat-out misfires. One thing you can never criticize Angel for is a lack of effort; the show never settled, never went for the easy payoff. It swung for the fences and even though it struck out a few times, the effort was always there and always felt. It's that reason why its fans, loyal and few though we be, stuck with the show from the rocky start, through the amazing middle, to the rushed and abrupt studio-mandated ending.

Let's talk about the rocky start.

Angel's first season can best be divided into two unequal halves. There's the first half, consisting of the season's initial ten episodes, and then there's everything else that followed, in the season's final twelve. The first ten episodes are built around what was likely intended to be the permanent core trio of castmates: Angel, Cordelia, and Doyle. Two of those are well-known to Buffy fans.

The titular character was part of some of Buffy's most important moments in her first three years, and her relationship with the vampire with a soul was the catalyst for Buffy's series to take the next step from "okay show with promise" to "must-see TV."

Nevertheless, after dying the way he did at the end of Buffy season 2, Angel was brought back with the writers forced to answer the question: How do you top what we've already done with Buffy/Angel? Angel returned early in Buffy season three and never really felt "in place." Of course, the only reason he was brought back was because his own series was already in development, but still, for most of Buffy's third year, Angel felt like he had one foot out the door, ready to go off and do his own thing, no longer defined simply as "Buffy's beau."

Cordelia on Buffy was, at first, nothing more than the cliche'd high school foil. She was the preppy, rich, stuck up popular girl who made life miserable for the new kid in town. Within just two and a half years, Cordy grew in a fully-realized character, and despite only having half the amount of screentime (if that) as the core Scooby gang, she arguably demonstrated more character development in those three seasons than anyone else in the entire show. Choosing her to leave to spread her wings on a new series was the perfect move by Joss Whedon.

The newcomer of the group is Doyle, and from the jump he never really fit. It's easy to say he wasn't given a fair shake due to his being the only one of the three that we didn't know, but the real problem was his character was too similar to Angel's.

Doyle a tormented demon, trying to do right in a world that is evil enough even without the supernatural ghouls running around. That's...basically Angel's whole schtick, and while it might've been interesting to introduce a character like that three or four years down the line, after Angel has developed and evolved, it doesn't work to bring him in for the pilot episode.

Fortunately, Joss and co. were unafraid to upset the applecart midway through a season; they wrote Doyle out in what was, ironically, the character's best episode, and spent the rest of the year developing the Angel/Cordy dynamic, building up the show's supporting cast of characters, and bringing in a new "third character" to complete the core cast.

Wesley Windham Price.

Introduced in Buffy season 3 as Faith's Watcher as well as a foil for Giles and overall a comic relief character/bumbling idiot, Wesley Windham Price takes the cake for greatest character development in the history of the Buffyverse. Other than maybe Star Trek: DS9's Damar, there's not another character in fiction who so smoothly and realistically goes from a glorified nobody to one of the most endearing somebodies on his show.

We'll say more about Wes as the series progresses, but in season one he is here simply to take the place of Doyle and when he does, instantly the show picks up in quality. There's a vibrancy, a fun energy, and a more comfortable dynamic at work whenever the trio of Angel,

MATTHEW L. MARTIN

Cordy, and Wes are on the screen together. Much of the second half of Angel is just as messy as the first, in terms of episode-by-episode plots, but getting through them is infinitely easier than it was when Doyle was playing the third wheel.

The less said about the episodes in Angel's first year the better. There are a few standouts, but the whole of it is just as clunky and stilted and uncertain of itself as you would expect from a debut season. Nevertheless, as with Buffy's first year, the episodes that work are the ones the creators learned from and replicated.

There are a handful of fun one-off episodes that matter very little other than being good compared to the stinkers: "Rm w/a vu" features Cordy contending with a ghost that's inhabiting a very nice and shockingly affordable apartment in L.A. "Somnambulist" sees Angel contend with a killer in town (played by a very young Jeremy Renner, about a dozen years before Joss would cast him as Hawkeye) that's copying a lot of his trademarks from his Angelus days.

The season finale "To Shanshu in L.A." is centered around an ancient prophesy (one which will define the character of Angel to the end) that says the vampire with a soul will die...or does it mean "become mortal"? Prophesies are tricky things.

But the real standouts this year center around the Slayers, Buffy and Faith. Angel's ex-girlfriend/forever-love comes to town early in the show's run (to give the fledgling series a ratings boost) in "I Will Remember You." It was only the eighth episode in the show's run, but it instantly launched to the top of the fan ratings and remained in the top ten until the end. It provided a fitting closure to the Buffy/Angel dynamic, packed in a ton of comedy and drama, and ended with an absolutely gut-punching final goodbye. Angel was created to be a more noir, darker, more brooding, more character-focused show than Buffy and no episode this season nailed that mission statement better than "I Will Remember You."

Faith's relationship with Angel—two good people who did a lot of bad and don't quite know how to deal with that fact—was never explored in Buffy and, sadly, wasn't explored nearly as much in Angel. Nevertheless, season one brought us a two-parter good enough to be a movie-of-the-week.

Faith awoke from her coma and did a lot of damage in two episodes of Buffy's fourth year, but she started to make amends in Sunnydale just before skipping town. Unfortunately, a lot of that amends-making was unbeknownst to Buffy, who tracked her down right as she was finally breaking down and wishing to die (a sentiment the ever-brooding Angel could easily identify and sympathize with). He takes her in right as Buffy arrives looking for a fight. What follows is a tense showdown between the old lovers, ending with Buffy essentially being told "this is my show town, we're doing things my way, go back to your show Sunnydale." It was just as much a declaration to the fans watching as it was to the characters: Angel is his own man, and his show will not be "Buffy 2.0"

And while, at times, it felt a lot like Buffy's first season 2.0, Angel's first season managed to reveal enough promise to make the whole endeavor something to come back to in year two. And just in case you needed extra motivation: Season one ends with the reveal that Darla—Angel's longtime vampire squeeze and partner in barbaric crime—has been resurrected.

Unlike Buffy, Angel loved to end seasons on a cliffhanger, and season one does just that, setting the stage for the title character to take his Buffy-sized leap in quality in season two.

Chapter Five

BUFFY SEASON FOUR

From the start, despite its rough bunch of early episodes, it's clear that Joss and co. knew its characters. The struggle was in figuring out what kinds of episodes to write to best highlight their personalities

In terms of the big picture, it was clear they were going for a "High School is hell...literally" parable, and never is that mantra more of the show's focus than in season one, where everything from social anxiety, depression, bullying, horny teachers, and more things that kids have to face in High School were tackled with a supernatural flare and plenty of teenage wise-cracking. The show was barely about vampires, despite the title character's primary role. The very episodic nature of the season, coupled with a lack of fan feedback until all episodes had been written and produced meant the series would need a second season to iron out the kinks, minimize what didn't work, and focus more on what did. The trouble was Buffy's ratings were not setting the world on fire, and the WB did not greenlight a second season until the very last minute.

Still, greenlight they did, and Joss and co. dove headfirst into season two now armed with the confidence that they had a winner on their hands, albeit one that needed a little polish. The resulting season is one of the most drastic jumps in quality from one year to the next in genre TV history. It's one thing to say "iron out the kinks, minimize what didn't work, and focus more on what did" but it's easier said than done. Most shows slide into a rut almost immediately and never break out of it until it's too late and the cancellation hammer falls.

Buffy, however, was a show almost defined by how willing it was to try new things, to shed seemingly established ideas, and even to take what worked and reshape it just to see if it could work under different circumstances. The season's biggest improvement was the addition of serialized elements, particularly with the Angel/Angelus arc, which carried the second half of the season and gave every episode, even the one-offs, a throughline that kept the audience invested on the road to the finale.

And what a finale it was. As said in the season two chapter, the finale featured a gut-wrenching dramatic finish that "earned" its ending thanks to weeks of buildup and with the help of writers that weren't afraid to make hard choices. The season ended with fans giddy to see what would happen next, and yet once again, the WB dragged its feet and left Joss and co. wondering if they would get a season three. Fortunately, at the eleventh hour, they did.

Season three is Buffy at its most confident. Joss and co. knew they had a potential winner in season one and knew how to craft it into a winner in season two. All that was left was to go out and put all the pieces together and present the best season yet. It's here where many shows falter; they run out of ideas or they get too comfortable repeating what worked until it becomes stale.

Never ones to keep things stagnant, Joss took advantage of the third season—the title character's senior year of high school—and treated it like the closing of a chapter. After two previous years not knowing if there would be next season, the team entered season three with the exact same thoughts, not knowing if there would be a season four, determined to leave it all on the line.

Joss has said in interviews that the constant uncertainty that surrounded the show's future meant he felt obligated to create season finales that could stand as "series" finales if it came to it. With Buffy entering her senior year of high school, Joss ended the year by literally blowing up the show, obliterating many of the locales we had come accustomed to seeing our heroes frequent, and graduating away (metaphorically and literally) at least two critical characters to the show's early success, Angel and Cordelia.

Buffy's third season was its most focused, its tightest, its cleverest, and its best written overall, climaxing with a finale that, had it been the actual end of the show, was still good enough to propel the series into cult hit status for years to come. Instead, fortunately, the show was once again renewed by the WB at the last minute, meaning Buffy and her friends would enter their fourth year together in an entirely new environment.

Buffy's fourth season is the most difficult one to rate. On the one hand it has, arguably, the largest collection of "best one-off episodes" in the series, while on the other hand, its overall arc is the weakest since season one (which basically didn't have an arc). As we've noted before, every

Buffy year tackles some aspect of maturation and adolescent development...

In season one, Buffy tackles her calling. In season two, it's her first love. In season three, it's the end of childhood that comes with a "graduation into adulthood." At least that's what everyone before they graduate always thinks, that they'll get their diploma and then suddenly boom, you're an adult. Nope. In reality, you're still the same person you were before, only now you're thrown into the deep end of the pool and forced to sink or swim. That messy aftermath of a graduation is the focus of season four; it tackles the awkward transition from being expected to be immature to demanded to be mature.

It's no surprise then that the two characters who best represented Buffy as a still-developing adolescent—Giles and her mother—see the biggest changes in their characters versus how they had been presented in seasons one through three. In the first three seasons, Buffy's mother was a recurring character there to make rules, give lectures, and "not understand" Buffy's grand calling. Typical mom stuff.

Giles, on the other hand, knew everything about Buffy's calling; he played the role of Merlin to her Arthur, mentoring her both as a quasi teacher and quasi father. The post-graduation life means the world expects you to make your own decisions more often and rely less on the counsel of parents. Buffy's mom is seen less than ever in this season, and Giles—a much more pivotal "character"—spends the year going through a kind of late-blooming mid-life crisis, wondering what to do with himself now that his library is blown up and his Slayer is off in college.

Oh yes. College.

Buffy season four never quite knew what to do with its college backdrop. Being at a university is radically different from being at High School. An incoming Freshman might think College is just "harder high school" but that's not it at all. It is harder, yes, but the real culture shock comes when you realize there are ten times as many kids on campus and literally none of them know who you are, or care, and the teachers aren't paid to coddle and quasi-parent you, either. You're on your own.

The writers of the show understood this, thankfully, so they didn't try to create a "high school 2.0" environment for the show. Instead, they used the college as a backdrop that just happened to be where various one-off episodes were set, and where the arc of the season was centered.

In fact, the show really only used its "college setting" to any great effect in one episode, the sublimely hilarious "Living Conditions" (4x02). Every other episode could have happened basically anywhere with only minimal changes, but "Living Conditions" depends entirely on Buffy being a Freshman at the University, forced to share a dorm room with "the roommate from Hell."

The best part about the episode is how the viewer is left to wonder for most of the runtime if Buffy's roommate really is a demon or if Buffy is just reacting to being an only child who suddenly has to share her "living conditions" with a peer. Granted, the roommate is a supremely annoying person, which leads to the greatest editing/camera gag in the series, when Buffy's roomie "borrows" her sweater and then drips ketchup on it. Buffy's reaction to this features one of the finest uses of the zoom feature in the history of film.

You can almost see the writers trying to work out what they want to do with the college setting within this one episode, as it ends with Willow moving in to be Buffy's roommate. It's a slight, mostly inconsequential outing, but it's also endlessly fun and is definitely going to be stupidly overrated by me when we get to the full episode-by-episode ranking.

But again, other than this one episode, the show never really made the college setting work, choosing instead to focus on Riley and the Initiative, a secret government division operating out of the college's secret underground basement, whose mission is to capture and experiment on various demons, vampires, and other supernatural ghouls that Buffy regularly interacts with.

The premise is fine but the execution suffers. A big part of the failure is the complete lack of credibility whenever these supposed military foot-soldiers are depicted doing "regular military stuff." When they bark orders, debate tactics, and run drills it's all so hokey and embarrassing. The writing is bad, the acting is worse, and the stark white rooms of their secret lair allow no visual flair to come through. Everything about this arc fell flat, and the writers knew it too, as they chose to wrap it up one episode before the finale, leaving the season's last episode to stand alone as something entirely different.

Speaking of stand-alone episodes, this is where Buffy's fourth season redeems itself. You want comedy? "Living Conditions." You want holiday fun? There's a great Halloween episode ("Fear, Itself") that sees the Scoobies trapped in a Haunted Frat house. There's also the wonderfully (admittedly, mildly tasteless) Thanksgiving episode ("Pangs") that sees the Scoobies haunted by the spirit of a Native American ghost.

Want a great two-parter? Faith returns for just that ("This Year's Girl/Who Are You"). Love seeing the background characters enjoy the spotlight? The perpetually picked-on Johnathan literally takes over an entire episode with hilariously surreal results ("Superstar").

Want hijinks? In "Something Blue" Willow casts a spell, accidentally (she's the show's Orko in that way) making her every statement be taken literally by whatever magical force grants her requests. As a result, Giles goes blind, Xander becomes a literal "demon magnet," and Buffy and Spike fall in love and decide to get married...leading to what is, perhaps, my favorite dialogue exchange in the entire show...

> *"What? How? What?"*
> - Xander

> *"Three excellent questions."*
> - Giles

But the real crown jewel of the season is "Hush." Going into this season, the show was regularly praised for its smart and sassy writing. During its run, Joss—whose career began as a writer and nothing else—used his powers as showrunner to get behind the camera and direct. In his own words, he used Buffy as his own personal film school.

Still, despite doing great work on episodes like "Prophesy Girl," "Becoming 1-2," and "Doppelgangland," he was always viewed as a "number one writer who sometimes directed," when he really wanted to be the show's number one "writer/director." Knowing his reputation as "the guy who writes all the great one-liners," Joss challenged himself to write and direct an episode that employed almost no dialogue.

"Hush" features a group of hauntingly designed monsters that suck the vocal abilities out of their enemies, rendering them mute while their still-beating hearts are cut out of their conscious bodies. The first segment of the episode proceeds like normal, but then "The Gentlemen" arrive and the show turns into a silent horror film.

This episode was, to this point, Joss' masterpiece, and it's only thanks to the sheer magnum opus achievement that is season six's "Once More with Feeling" that "Hush" is not the number one episode of the entire series (spoiler alert for the big "episode-by-episode ranking" at the end of this book). Without dialogue, the show relies on the physical presence of the actors and a great score by Christophe Beck, along with enough visual gags to keep the laughs going even without Whedon's typical quips and one-liners.

The one-off episodes this season carry the show, which is ironic as it was the overly-episodic nature of season one that held it back, and the powerful arcs in seasons two and three that propelled the show to greatness. Still, when the arc-heavy episodes this year stumbled almost every time they were given the spotlight, you could always count on a standalone gem to come along a week later to remind you why this show is one of the best.

As said, the failure of the arc was not lost on the creative team. Some of it was due to their own failure to make it work, while other challenges were forced on them, such as the sudden departure of the actress who was set to be the big bad for Buffy to have her showdown with. The deck had to be reshuffled, a new baddie had to be introduced late in the game, and the whole thing was rushed to a clumsy conclusion with one episode to spare.

To be fair, the arc's final episode, "Primeval" at least does as good a job as possible to wrap things up, and the climax—featuring Buffy drawing on the combined powers of Willow, Giles, and Xander to become a kind of Super Saiyan Buffy is really cool, but the less said about The Initiative arc, the better.

BUFFY THE VAMPIRE SLAYER

Needing something for a final episode, Joss Whedon crafted a surreal dream-centered episode called "Restless," which sees the four principal characters Buffy, Willow, Giles, and Xander, all fall asleep at Buffy's house during a "movie night hangout." The result is a series of dreams with writer/director Whedon doing his best send-up to David Lynch. The episode features some of the best depictions of the fractured, non-sequitur-filled experiences that come with dreaming ever put to film, TV or otherwise...

Going over all the prophesies and hints at future storylines filled in this episode would cover an entire chapter in its own right. Suffice to say, "Restless" might not put a capper on the season the way "Becoming 1-2" or "Graduation Day 1-2" did, but it did finish the season, fittingly, by making us forget all about the misfire of an arc and instead gave us a stellar one-off to end things on a high note.

As was customary, the WB Network kept Joss hanging until the last minute regarding renewal or cancellation. Thankfully, a fifth season was approved, and much as he did after learning from the mistakes of season one, Joss would set out to make the fifth season one that corrected the mistakes here and built on the successes, setting the stage for an upcoming year that fans would never forget.

MATTHEW L. MARTIN

Chapter Six

ANGEL SEASON TWO

Much like Buffy, Angel's first season was a rocky road. Unlike Buffy, the feeling-out process for Angel involved cast shake-ups and even a tweaking of the entire driving force of the show.

What started out as a pulpy, noir-heavy, detective story (with vampires), focusing on three core characters and a police detective/possible love interest on the side, became something very different by the end of season one. Gone was Doyle, the half-demon who received visions from "the powers that be" and guided Angel along

67

each episode's plot. Those duties were shuffled over to Cordelia, who, in turn, finally found a purpose to the overall thrust of the show. In Doyle's place was the returning Wesley Windham Price, a carryover from Buffy's third season, who worked on that show mostly as a comedic foil.

Wes' character is reintroduced to us in Angel in much the same way, though he quickly develops into a well-rounded character and a vital member of the cast (really, that's understating it; Wes has arguably the greatest character evolution in the entire Buffyverse). As the show finished its first season, the character of Police Detective Kate Lockley was still around, though her role was shrinking fast, and at the start of season two she was basically a bit part no more important than Joyce in the fourth season of Buffy.

To put it mildly, the season that began with "City Of" was not the same show that ended with "To Shanshu in L.A." It had grown in quality and proved its willingness to shake up its rules and foundations in order to get the best product on the screen. It also ended with the promise that things were going to get a whole lot wilder in year two, as the overarching baddies of Wolfram & Hart devised a way to resurrect Angel's old squeeze, Darla.

Season two thus begins with the promise that the writers had worked out the kinks and were ready to dive deeper into the mythology and character development they only teased in season one. It wouldn't be the same show, but it would still be Angel. That tone is set immediately, as the first thing we see is a green-skinned and red-horned demon emerging from stage-right amidst spooky lighting.

He then proceeds to sing karaoke.

Lorne is just one of a trio of characters either introduced to us this season or who are promoted to series regulars. Lorne, to put it simply, is too good for this world. He's a demon with a love for performing, a perennially happy disposition, and a desire to please. On the one hand, he's exactly the kind of character that the network would request be added to the show, to bring some brightness to it, but on the other, he's just the kind of cat that Joss Whedon would proactively envision.

Think about it: What crucial skills or qualities does Lorne bring to the mix? He can't (and won't) fight. He has no great wealth. He has no important connection to any hero or villain in the show. He's purely ancillary, and other than being an empath who can sing, he can't really do anything. And yet, I can't imagine this show without him. In a show as dark and brooding as this one often got in year one (even the light-hearted episodes were often gloomy), Lorne strutted into season two like a Christmas-colored breath of fresh air. He might not do anything, but his mere delightful presence alone is enough to warrant keeping him around.

Another face that we only just started getting to know in year one is Gunn, who appeared in the final three episodes of the first season. Starting with season two, he's added as a show regular and given billing in the opening credits, something that will become the norm in Angel (every new season features someone new added to the credits).

While Angel works as a warrior of a different era, and Wesley is a very book-oriented fighter, Gunn is depicted as the man getting his hands dirty, doing real fighting in the streets. He brings a different dimension than we'd gotten to this point in the Buffyverse but it took the writers a year or so before they figured out exactly how to present his character. Early on he's too much of a caricature, and the episodes focusing on him rarely land in the upper echelon of the show.

Fortunately, most of season two revolves around the toxic relationship between Angel and Darla, and it's here where the show shines.

In one of the show's best recurring vignettes, Angel regularly flashes back to ancient times, when Angelus, Darla, Spike, and Drusilla, trotted from country to country wreaking havoc and feasting on all manner of innocents. We'd heard a lot about how evil Angelus was in his former days, and we certainly got a taste of it in Buffy's second season, but it was only here that we are actually shown what made this foursome the most feared vampires in the world.

The flashbacks serve a purpose, however, as they inform us of the inner-thoughts Angel is wrestling with while dealing with the resurrected Darla. In what is easily the series' best story arc, lasting two seasons, Joss and co. take the viewers on a journey with more twists, surprises, and layers than any other long-told story on either show. This season is basically divided into two mini-arcs, with a final arc at the end of the season that's detached from the Angel/Darla drama.

At first, Angel sees Darla around Los Angelus, and suspects he's crazy, seeing a ghost. When he finally confronts the woman, she acts as if she doesn't know him and flees, escaping from him into the sunlight. Later, Angel tracks her down to a home where she appears to be a normal housewife, a mere look-alike to the woman he was with for literal centuries. Then the first twist happens: Darla, we learn, was resurrected with a mortal soul, but that carried with it a resurrection of all the mortal ailments her former self once had. Before becoming a vampire, Darla was a prostitute and was dying of syphilis.

Choosing immortality over certain death, Darla became a vamp, met up with Angel and the rest is history. Now that she's back so too is her fatal disease, too far along to be cured with modern medicine. She begs for Angel to turn her back into a vampire, which he naturally refuses. Instead, he embarks on a quest to save her life.

Under normal circumstances, the hero would prevail, but no: Twist #2 is that Angel fails and Darla remains doomed to die. The two embrace and accept their fate before—shock of shocks and one of the best moments in all of Buffy or Angel—Drusilla makes her return and does the deed Angel would not. With one bite, the old Darla is back and we begin the next mini-arc of the season, as Darla and Drusilla go on a tear.

Bitter and angry over everything that's happened, Angel sinks into a dark inner place, fires his team, and goes bad (not Angelus bad, but bad enough to rattle the vampires he's hunting). This culminates in twist #3: Angel sleeping with Darla. As lightning crashes in the aftermath, we're led to believe that Angelus has returned, but no: Angel's soul only leaves when he experiences true happiness, something a one-off with Darla can't create. The brief dalliance brings Angel back to the light and he returns to the team he fired, asking to work for them. This takes us into the final arc of the season, as the Darla-drama is put on hold so we can spend some time in Lorne's demon dimension.

For most of it, Angel's second season was just as heavy, dramatic, and dark as the first, but the character-interaction kept it from being too dour, and the long-form plot-twisty arc (which season one didn't have) kept its viewers perpetually hooked. Fans who stuck with the season over the course of its first sixteen episodes, were treated to the first half of an epic tale, the rest of which would play out during the show's third year.

Before that, however, and after a few one-off episodes to tie up loose ends, Angel's second year ended with a visit to Pylea, the medieval, war-loving land where everyone who looks like Lorne acts like the monster we assumed Lorne to be when we first laid eyes on him. These final episodes of the season offer a happy detour from the darkness experienced previously; it's a reward to the fans who endured such a grim and heavy storyline, and most importantly, it provides us with the character that will come to be the series' heart and soul: Winifred Burkle.

More on her later.

Angel's second year was not as flashy as Buffy's sophomore outing. It didn't have the great one-off episodes nor a singular tone-shifting moment akin to what Angel turning into Angelus brought to Buffy's year two. That would be a regular struggle the show would live with for the duration of its time on the air: It was never as flashy as Buffy and always put more emphasis on the slow-burn arc and character development than it did having a really memorable plot every week.

Buffy's episodes are best considered in single offerings, and occasionally as two-parters. Angel, on the other hand, is a series of arcs, with the occasional one-off that rises above the rest. It makes it harder to compare to its sister show but, as Joss Whedon famously quipped, "Angel was the one show on the WB that was trying not to be Buffy."

The series never hit the ratings mark that its companion series reached, but those who stuck with Angel will swear by the show's high quality, and often praise it as some of the best character writing in all of Joss and co.'s TV wheelhouse. A big reason for that praise is the work done, not only in the excellent second season, but also in the year that followed.

MATTHEW L. MARTIN

Chapter Seven

BUFFY SEASON FIVE

Buffy's first year was a show still figuring itself out, still learning how to tell the kinds of stories its writers—namely Joss Whedon—wanted, and still fine-tuning the balance between silly and serious, a balance that started out somewhere in the 90% silly/10% serious range before settling down to a healthy 75% silly/25% serious ratio for the epic season one finale.

I say "epic" in comparison to the episodes before it. In every way, however, Buffy's second season would outdo its first. It was bolder, more confident, more risky, more audacious, more dramatic, and more silly than anything that came in year one. This was the season, in particular the two-parter "Surprise/Innocence," that figured out the groove that the show would run in for the remainder of its time on television.

But that's not to say the show ever got stale. On the contrary, while the formula was perfected, Joss and co. refused to rest on their laurels, and instead blew up (literally) the primary setting for the show at the end of year three.

After a high-stakes season that saw the introduction of a new Slayer (on account of Buffy temporarily dying in the season one finale), and the advent of a monstrous demon prepped to consume the entire high school graduation, Buffy and pals saved the day by slaying the monster and exploding the school into a million-and-one pieces. With the premise of the show built around the phrase "high school is hell...literally," and with your heroine graduating from said high school...where do you go from here?

To college, apparently. Buffy and the gang stayed in town but shifted to the world of higher education. Unfortunately, as we noted in our season four review, this was the year when the show proved its excellent writers were not always able to spin straw into gold.

The college setting failed to provide as much creative fuel as being in high school, and other than a few moments here and there (and not all of them good; see "beer bad"), year four saw the writers realize they couldn't make college work. To their credit, they didn't try to force it, either. They didn't go so far as to blow up the university, but they did shift the storytelling focus to the interpersonal drama, which was always Buffy's strong suit anyway.

The only setback in that regard was the character of Riley, and the storyline-of-boredom known as "The Initiative." Riley offered Buffy Summers a stable, normal relationship. It was intentionally boring and safe, but that only made the boyfriend at the center of it come off as boring and safe (not to mention hokey to a fault whenever forced to spew the 'pretend army' dialogue he was hamstrung with).

While the writers were in top form whenever free to let their creativity run wild, the season was regularly held back by the Riley/Initiative storyline. The result is a fourth season that has some of the absolute best standalone episodes in the series, while being saddled with the weakest season-long arc in all of Buffy.

As the writers headed into year five they did so with a few things dangling in front of them. First, was the challenge to fix the mistakes made in the fourth season. Second, was the fact that the five-year contract, that most of the key figures involved in the show had signed when it began, was coming to an end.

As we've noted in previous chapters, Buffy had the grim reaper hanging over it every spring as the final episode of each season hit the airwaves. Most big network shows were renewed long before the season finale aired, but WB regularly made Joss and co. wait until the eleventh hour to renew the show for a new season. Because of that, Joss made sure each finale worked as a potential "final episode ever," just in case the network ended up passing on the show after filming was done.

Season one ended with Buffy embracing her destiny and becoming the Slayer she was always meant to be. If that had been the end, it would have been a neat and tidy bow on a fun little half-season.

Season two ended with Buffy killing her beloved to save the world, and then leaving to start a new life. Had that been the end, it would have been a poignant close to a show about sacrifice and loss and the price we pay to be a hero.

Season three ended, as said, with the newly graduated Buffy blowing up the school and saying goodbye to many of her friends as they went their separate ways. Of all of them, this would have been the most fitting "series finale," had it come to that.

Even the helter-skelter season four ended with the sublime and surreal "Restless," an episode that explored the dreams of the show's four most important characters, and ended with the vague promise that Buffy's most important days were still ahead of her. Had that been the end, well it would have been a blue baller of a finish, but it would have left us wondering the way many final chapters often do.

Now we come to season five, and never has there been a year where "this might be our last" was more contemplated. The need to tie up loose ends is all over this year's batch of episodes, as is the need to go out (potentially) with a bang, and bring some sort of closure to the journey the show had been on for the past half-decade. It's no spoiler now, a quarter-century later, to say that Buffy will, in fact, get another season (two, actually), but that was not known at the time, and the result is a season that works, much like season three, as the closing of a chapter, and a fitting end to the story of Buffy Summers...

Season five begins with an episode that feels like the start of something, only for it to end up a punchline. That's a common criticism of the Joss Whedon school of writing, that he always undercuts his dramatic or important moments with a gag or a quip. I get it, and you can certainly cite many examples of it, but it's not entirely fair to cast this as his big sin as a writer.

There are scores of episodes that let the dramatic moments play out without any levity: Buffy's "I don't want to die" speech in the season one finale, her killing Angel at the end of season two, or her beautiful recognition at the Prom in season three, just to name a few.

The reason many complain that Joss never lets a sad or special moment breathe is because many of the moments that fans expect to be sadder or more important simply aren't that important to the writer in charge. In episode one this year, Buffy faces off against the most famous vampire of them all: Dracula. The episode's title is the perfectly succinct "Buffy vs. Dracula." You expect fireworks. You expect this to kick off a multi-episode arc. You might even think the big man himself will be the big bad of the whole season.

Instead she dusts him in a one-off episode.

Granted, Dracula comes back (he can't be dusted like the rest of the vamps for reasons left unexplained)...but Buffy just waits there so she can stab him again, etc. It's a gag and it matters none at all. If you thought this was the beginning of something remarkable, well...maybe stop worrying about the show being what you want it to be and just let it be what it is. Season five doesn't begin with the introduction of the big bad (actually, it does, we just don't realize it yet). It begins with a lot of fun as Buffy proves she's at the top of her game by taking down the most famous vampire of them all. She's at the top, which means the only thing to do is knock her down. And that's what this season does: It strips away Buffy's sense of her own heroism.

To this point, Buffy has saved the day many times over by using her brains and brawn, whether it's taking down a monster "that cannot be killed with sword or stake" by blowing it up with a rocket launcher, or running her lover through with a sword to stop the apocalypse, Buffy will do what it takes to get the "win," and thus far she's got a pretty great record of wins notched on her belt. So what happens when you give her a challenge she can't "beat"? What happens when she's forced to accept that sometimes you can't win every fight, and she has to choose between failure as a fighter, or success as a sacrifice?

That sacrifice is centered around a new character to the Buffy universe: Dawn. Reviled at first, only to grow as a character and end the series as a vital component, Dawn is introduced to us here, first as an enigma. The writers were certainly not the first to tackle bringing in a new character to a well-established show, but in this case, instead of finding some contrived "uncle Billy is moving in with us" or "cousin Freddie is moving into town and will, conveniently, be hanging around our house from now on" way of handling the changeup, the writers of Buffy worked out an in-universe solution: Wizard monks did it.

Instead of making Dawn's role in the season an appendage that fans would either love or hate, Joss and his writers made her the lynchpin of the season's entire arc. She is "the key" that the big bad of year five is after to unlock the portal to her dimension (that, upon opening, will unleash hell on earth).

Once upon a time, this "key" was nothing more than a ball of energy. Desperate to keep it out of the hands of the big bad, the monks took that ball of energy and formed it into a person, then altered the entire fabric of reality and placed her in the Summers home, leading Buffy and her mother (and everyone else, including Dawn) to believe that she is Buffy's little sister who has been a part of their lives...from the beginning.

Early in the season, no one questions Dawn's placement: Buffy groans about her kid sister. Xander acts as a surrogate big brother.

MATTHEW L. MARTIN

Willow and Tara (especially Tara) offer the kind of sweet "big sisterly love" that Buffy takes for granted. And Joyce, the mother, acts exactly like the loving (if a bit overprotective) mother she's always been.

The writing is so underappreciated here in how well they slid the Dawn character in so that everyone acts as though she's always been around. It's only the audience that is left in the dark, with some feeling gaslighted, wondering about past episodes, trying to recall if there was any mention of Dawn before now, if she was talked about but never seen.

Indeed she was talked about, but only in the form of prophesy. In fact, two years before the season five finale, Buffy has a prophetic dream that involves Faith mentioning "little Miss Muffet" and a countdown to the big "7-3-0."

Understanding the latter informs us of the former: There were exactly 730 days from the end of season three to the end of season five, and already Joss Whedon had in his mind that year five, should he get one, would end with Buffy sacrificing herself to save a little sister she didn't even know she had. How the season gets to that point, however, revolves around two things. Remember, Buffy's seasons are always about two things: There is always an internal and an external driving force to the stories/arcs:

BUFFY THE VAMPIRE SLAYER

Every Buffy season explores a key aspect of life and maturity befitting the title character's age and development. In season one, Buffy tackles her calling. In season two, it's her first love. In season three, it's the end of childhood. In season four, it's the awkward transition between being immature and mature. In season five, it's the grim realities of adulthood.

The internal struggle this year, about dealing with the realities of adulthood, is tackled, outwardly, through the challenges posed by the season's big bad. And who is this big bad? Let's take a moment to appreciate the prior big bad villains of the show thus far.

In season one, Buffy faced off against a Nosferatu-looking vampire with a hard-on for killing her: The Master was the perfect, most quintessential, "first boss" for our heroine to conquer, especially in a year whose internal theme revolved around her answering the call of her heroic destiny.

In season two, she had to take on her lover, laying the drama on thick and perfectly tying in with the internal theme of dealing with the drama of your first serious love interest.

In season three, as the heroine prepared to graduate from high school and take her first steps into the wider world, it's fitting that she would have to take down a demon in the guise of a mild-mannered, even affable, "guy in a business suit" that secretly is the worst.

In season four, as she tackled the transition to maturity, she had to take down the Government itself, and the inept way the bureaucrats tried to do Buffy's job (and screwed it all up)...which is exactly the kind of persistent nuisance that will plague adults for the rest of their lives but which a child would have no concept of.

So, in season five, with the realities of adulthood and the certainty that you can't win-em-all hanging over her, who better to embody that challenge than...

A valley girl?!

No, really, it's perfect. Glory is perfect. She's actually a god from another dimension with more power than any baddie before her. The whole "valley girl princess" schtick is just the embodiment of her vanity, which makes perfect sense considering her god-like nature.

She is a frequently worshipped, often monologuing, regularly air-headed, brain-sucking god of mayhem with zero regard for human life. All she wants is to find one little key that will let her go back to the dimension she was kicked out of, even if that means spilling the worst of that dimension out into our world to do it. Millions will die? Billions? What is that to a god?

Obviously, there's a lot going on this year, including a ton of character development for Spike, as he teeters on the edge of a full-blown turn from likeable villain to lovable good guy. There's also the continuing romance between Xander and Anya which makes for some delightful and hilarious moments. And there's Riley, who gets half a season to bumble around and be perfectly cromulent in all the worst possible ways.

But the real heart of the season, excluding our big bad, revolves around three women, the Summers: Buffy, Dawn, and Joyce...

After seeing her role diminish with each successive season, Buffy's mother Joyce returns in a big way in season five. Obviously, there was a plan at work from the beginning of the year, so giving her more screen-time made sense, but we didn't know about any plan at the beginning of the season.

And yet, Joyce's return to semi-regular status makes perfect sense for a couple of different reasons. For one, Buffy is no longer living at the dorm (another not-so-subtle allusion to the failures of season four), so of course we would see her mom around more with Buffy at home more. For another, with Dawn coming into the family, it made logical sense for Joyce to be there, mothering (helicopter-parenting) the younger sibling just as she once did Buffy.

Buffy's perspective toward her mother was different this year as well. She was much warmer toward her, less put-out by her out of touch and naïve ways. Again, there was an endgame to all this, but we didn't know it at the time.

At the time this all made sense considering where Buffy was as a character: She was graduated and transitioning into proper adulthood. Naturally she would see her mother differently as her mother would treat her differently. They would start to become more sisterly, each sharing the responsibility of raising young Dawn (something Dawn herself would naturally resent). It all fit together, neat and tidy, and if that's all that came of it, it still would be regarded as solid writing.

But, as you know, there was more to it.

Early in the season, Joyce starts suffering from headaches and fainting spells. A trip to the hospital (and a chat with the new doctor character Ben, who has nothing to do with Glory or anyone so let's forget about him) informs us that Joyce has a tumor in her brain. Instantly— knowing that Joss Whedon derives more pleasure out of making audiences cry than anything else in his life—fans took to assuming the worst, counting down the days until Joyce would bite the dust.

What's great, and I mean how it's a masterstroke of patient writing, is the way Joss stretched out the inevitable to the point where fans started to think everything maybe was going to be okay. In the meanwhile, fans at the time frequently joked about the prospects of Joyce's death, not because the character was unliked (not anymore; season five brilliantly rehabbed her character), but just because it was fun to think about all the ways Joss would torture the viewers. We weren't emotionally invested in the idea of losing Joyce, and when the brain tumor ended up being benign and Joyce started to mend, viewers were quick to move to the next plot device, letting their guard down...

And then we lost Joyce.

Once again, and this too was a masterstroke, is the way they landed the first reveal of Joyce's death. It happens at the end of a light-hearted, silly, one-off episode. Do people even remember that? Do you remember the one where some rando nerdy robot-builder saw one of his creations (a robot girlfriend) go wild on Sunnydale? It's a funny but slight episode. I rank it almost in the exact middle of the series, #65 out of 131. It's good but hardly memorable, especially when compared to the episode that came next.

We may forget, that the episode ends with the sight of Joyce lying dead, out of focus, on the living room couch, as Buffy comes home from saving the day yet again. It ends with her pained, fragile, pleading of "mom...mom...mommy..." before the screen fades to black.

To this point in the season, if not the whole series, Buffy has won every battle. She was killed by the master but shrugged it off and came back. She had to kill her lover, but he returned a few months later. She stopped the Mayor, took out the Initiative, defeated Dracula, has kept Dawn safe from Glory, and on the list goes. Even when it comes to her mother, we've already had the tumor scare. Buffy was powerless and helpless there but, in the end, Joyce recovered, making the heroine no doubt feel like a champion all over again. She's a winner. Everything's going her way. And then she (and we, the viewers) sees the body.

The episode is called "The Body," and it's one of the most gut-wrenching, raw, and realistic depictions of the whirlwind that follows the death of a family member that you'll ever find on any TV series, in any genre, anywhere, ever. It holds up so brilliantly today that it can be appreciated by someone who has never seen an episode, has no context or background in the series, and just turns this on without any set-up. It is essentially a short film by Joss Whedon, made to explore grief, loss, and the frustration and helplessness one feels when faced with the finality of death.

The whole structure of the episode is perfect. Joss Whedon (writer/director) knew the best way to sell the impact was to show how Joyce's death affected everyone, so he gives everyone not only a big moment but a mini-arc for how they process it...

Willow is self-conscious about how to help Buffy, Anya is frustrated because as an ex-demon that's lived for countless ages but has never been close to a mortal before, she doesn't understand the feelings of loss she's experiencing, Giles leaps into "parent mode" and refuses to process her death so he can focus on Buffy (until the next episode when he's shown playing records that he and Joyce listened to in the episode "Band Candy"), Tara thinks about how best to use her own mother's death to help the grievers, Xander looks for something to get angry at, and Dawn remains in denial throughout the episode, insisting on seeing the body because it's not real till she does.

Buffy is actually given the least to do once you get past the absolutely devastating opening.

MATTHEW L. MARTIN

After that, she withdraws entirely within herself, which we later learn is her way of dealing with the loss: As long as she's planning the funeral and making decisions she never has to say goodbye and move on.

It's just a fantastically put-together episode, presented without any soundtrack, with very very few jokes (and the ones we get are contextually appropriate, as anyone who has gone through this whirlwind will tell you, humor naturally slips out at unexpected times), and other than a moment in the morgue, without any grappling with the undead.

This is the episode that slaps Buffy hard in the face with the realization that she is fallible, that she can't win every battle and walk away with a shrug on her shoulder and a quip on her lips. to say that she is never the same after this is an understatement: The loss of Buffy's mother, and the way she processes it, will reverberate, especially throughout the rest of the season.

Because we still have a "rest of the season."

The death of Joyce happens only two-thirds of the way through year five, and just as Buffy is only starting to move back to a kind of normalcy, Glory figures out that Dawn is the key and the heroes are forced to go on the run. By this point, Glory has already driven Tara insane and by the end of the two-parter "Tough Love/Spiral," Glory has beaten Buffy and kidnapped Dawn, intending to kill her to open the portal that will unleash her dimension on earth. That's a series of defeats that have hit our heroine in very short order.

I didn't even mention the departure of Riley earlier this year, which I suppose can be categorized as a loss (even if I see it as an absolute win). Never has Buffy been so outmatched and overwhelmed before. As a result, at the end of "Spiral," she suffers a nervous breakdown and collapses, forcing Willow to enter her mind in the underrated episode "The Weight of the World," and bring her back to fight again.

"The Weight of the World" is not regarded highly in the Buffy fandom, but it serves an important purpose, to explore the inner mindset of a hero that is only now forced to confront the reality of losing. It is both a perfectly logical result of everything that has happened thus far, and a critical set-up to what will happen in the finale.

It's also a reminder of the kind of TV content that is quickly going by the wayside: Most TV series of any acclaim are released in eight to thirteen episode chunks, featuring stripped-down, plot-heavy storylines that don't allow much time for the kind of silly, trippy, or otherwise experimental one-off episodes that made Buffy so great. You couldn't get an episode like "The Zeppo" in a Netflix season. An episode like "Restless" would never have been made to close out an eight-episode season on Disney+; they would have finished the arc with the Initiative, in all its "meh," and swallowed the disappointment without ending on a high note.

A protracted season allows you to have a higher budget and a tighter overall storyline, but you lose the small bursts of creativity that come from an episode like "The Weight of the World," where Willow and Buffy have an existential conversation in the recesses of her mind, ending with Buffy confessing that, after all that's happened, she finally has come to believe that she can't win; she can't beat Glory. Willow, however, shames her for refusing to try. That snaps Buffy out of it, and the episode ends with the hero ready to do whatever it takes, even losing, just for the chance of saving the day.

Which takes us to "The Gift."

Not to spoil things, but it's worth mentioning that five of Buffy's seven finales rank in the top ten of my "every Buffy episode ranked" listing (coming early next year), and "The Gift" is the second-highest rated of those finale episodes (behind "Becoming 1-2"). It is another Joss Whedon episode but, unlike his more experimental outings like "Restless," or "Hush," or "The Body," this one is more traditional, in the mold of "Graduation Day 1-2." It highlights the writer/director's ability to tie up loose ends, make effective callbacks, payoff long-awaited moments, and leave the audience both satisfied and begging for more.

"The Gift" is a marvelous episode and has the most "final episode" feel of all the finales thus far, likely because, at this point, the team in front and behind the camera didn't know if UPN would buy the rights to a sixth and seventh season, and The WB had all but indicated they were done with the show. This was, as far as they could plan it, the end.

And what an end it was.

Everyone gets a moment, including (1) Giles who brings out a bit of the old Ripper in him, (2) Xander, who proposes to Anya, (3) Willow and Tara, who have a killer moment where they wordlessly cast a spell that gives Spike an avenue to get to Dawn, and (4) Spike, who almost saves the day like the hero he didn't know he was becoming...before he fails.

Spike fails, Buffy fails, everyone fails. Glory's plan was to drain Dawn's blood to open the portal and once it's opened, the only way to stop it is to kill Dawn, something Buffy—having already lost her mother—refuses even to consider. Dawn might not have actually lived with her for all those years, but in her mind, she had, and at that point what's the difference? Buffy thinks of Dawn as her sister so she is her sister, and now she stands on the catwalk, with Dawn dripping blood over a slowly opening portal and the only solution is to kill her.

And that's when Buffy has her epiphany...

The episode ends with Buffy, realizing she can't win this one and walk away with a quip, deciding to win it by sacrificing, not her sister, but herself. The fact that this realization comes while she beholds the dawn (of a new day), just before dying to save her Dawn is too perfect for words. She leaps to her death, closing the portal and earning a tombstone whose engraving brings a hiccup of laughter and happy tears amidst all the ugly crying:

Buffy Anne Summers.
1981-2001
SHE SAVED THE WORLD,
A LOT.

Her final words to Dawn include this beautifully poignant line, "The hardest thing in this world is to live in it," words that will come back to her when she again contemplates taking her own life, not as a heroic sacrifice, but as a desperate suicide to escape the hardships that had befallen her. But that's a story for another season, and we'll talk about season six later.

In the meantime, Buffy wasn't the only one going through big changes. Angel was too, as evidenced throughout his second season and into his third...

Chapter Eight

ANGEL SEASON THREE

Angel's third season felt very much like an extension of the second. There was a clear and obvious shift in the way the show told its stories in season two as compared to season one, and other than the Darla tease at the end of the first finale, there wasn't much carry-over, either.

Season two, on the other hand, left a ton of unanswered questions and unresolved plot points. Darla was still out there, as was Drusilla. Instead of wrapping up those matters, the final few episodes of the year went in a completely different direction, detouring us to the demon realm of Lorne. Everyone comes home by the end of the year, bringing with them Winifred Burkle, and the season ends with the news that Buffy had died. We're not told how that announcement affected Angel, but we can guess.

As season three opens, the events here run in parallel to the happenings of Buffy season six, so it won't be for a few weeks before Angel learns Buffy is alive again. In the meantime he spends his summer in Sri Lanka, trying to meditate and ease the hurt. All he ends up finding there are a bunch of demonic monks, so he packs up and returns home to find comfort by keeping busy and taking his mind off the loss of his love. Goal #1 is helping Fred integrate into the group and the world at large.

Despite being introduced to us at the end of the last season, it's really only here where we get a real sense of who this new Fred character will be. To put it simply, she's pure bliss. She's an endlessly happy, wicked smart, southern girl from Texas, with a smile that steals every scene, and a pluckiness that never (ever) grates on the nerves.

Do you know how hard it is to have a character as relentlessly optimistic and "just happy to be here" as she is without her ever becoming public enemy #1 with the fans? Not only does Fred avoid that, but she manages to pull off being a fan favorite that didn't come in until halfway through the show's entire run. It's a testament to how quickly the writers nailed her character and how effortlessly the actress in question—Amy Acker—walked the line between earnest and charming.

Anytime a new character joins a TV show, you can expect several episodes to focus on them, as sort of a character development speed-run to get them on the same level of familiarity as the rest of the cast. Thus, Fred gets quite a bit of screentime this season, and more than a few B-plots centered around her. She's not the driving force of the year however, and in fact, neither is Angel.

The real centerpiece, through which the main arc of the year is constructed, is the other new character introduced to us this year: Daniel Holtz. While he's not a cast-regular, and only appears in half the episodes this season, he nevertheless drives the plot. His character is just the kind of Big Bad that Angel's show has needed from the outset. Thus far, he's contended with run-of-the-mill monsters and ghouls, and tangled with an evil law firm, but at its core, the character Angel is about a man haunted by his past.

Angelus was the most feared and ruthless vampire in history, "cursed" into goodness, and now forced to live with the shame of his prior evil. The drama that comes with that has certainly been explored from an internal perspective, but other than listening to Darla yearn from those "good old days" there really hasn't been much of an exploration of Angel's past external to the man himself.

Enter Daniel Holtz: A vampire hunter from the late-1700s, he was arguably the greatest non-supernatural slayer in history. Ten years into his very successful work, much of which was consumed by chasing (and failing to slay) Angel and Darla, he came home to find his wife and child killed by Angel and his daughter turned into a vampire by Darla. Thus began a quest for vengeance that completely consumed him.

Despite his zeal, he failed repeatedly to capture the vamps. Eventually, he became a hermit before the time-shifting demon Sahjhan found him. The demon essentially offered him the chance to live forever until the right time presented itself when he could pay Angelus back for all he did. Fast forward 200 years and it's the year 2001, Angelus is now Angel and Holtz is back and looking for retribution. It does not matter to him that Angel is reformed; he's too broken to be swayed by such nuance.

Here's a character that, on paper, is easy to root against as a traditional villain. Instead, the way he is depicted, you almost feel sorry for him. Angelus did commit unspeakable evil to him, enough to drive him beyond reason. He is the perfect adversary for the show's protagonist: He's a monster of the hero's own making. And under the circumstances of a lesser show, this year would have been about the cat and mouse between these two, ending in some heartbreaking death for the "villain" that tears Angel up inside. Clean and simple.

But that's not this show.

This show insists on twisting the knife and throwing in surprises you never saw coming at you. The big one this year is revealed to us at the end of the first episode: Darla is extremely pregnant. We're not yet told who the daddy is, but we're also not stupid. There's only one man it could be to create maximum drama.

We learn in episode two the father is another vampire and that such a pregnancy is completely inconceivable among the undead. After that, we get several episodes of radio silence, while Fred is better introduced to us. But episode seven brings the major arc of the season roaring back, with a three-episode stretch that shows just how confident and polished the show had become in such a brief period of time.

In episode seven, Darla returns and reveals her condition to Angel, at the same time Holtz is awakened from his 200-year nap, looking to kill.

In episode eight, Holtz brings the fight to Angel and nearly takes him out, at the same time Darla's water breaks. In episode nine, we discover that Darla is unable to deliver the child naturally (on account of her being undead and all) and her body is too strong for a C-section to work. The not-delivery will kill them both so, in what is her finest and most selfless moment, Darla stakes herself, turning to dust in Angel's arms, leaving him holding the baby in her wake.

It's a whirlwind trio of episodes that never slows down, where every installment ends with a cliffhanger to leave you breathless, and where the closing moment serves as a tour de force for Whedon and co as TV creators. As well-constructed as season two was overall, these three episodes stand head and shoulders over everything else.

Angel slows down after Connor is born, and we're given half a dozen episodes that reset the table and bring the tension back down to zero. It doesn't stay that way, however. The final third of the season, beginning with episode fifteen's "Loyalty," kicks off the character arc that will come to define Wesley Windham Price, completing his transition from "joke character" to "key member of the team" to, finally, "baddest dude ever."

Wesley's character transformation begins subtly enough, with him discovering ancient texts prophesying that Angel will kill Connor. Typical Wesley stuff. His investigation leads him to one of those things you just have to see to believe: He goes to an ancient mystic in the guise of a giant hamburger-shaped fast-food drive-thru speaker box.

This is a thing that happened and I will never **not** stare blankly at the screen every time this scene happens.

Anyway, the giant hamburger man tells Wesley that the prophesy is true and "the father will devour the son," whatever that means. One episode later, Wesley, convinced that he's doing the right thing, steals Connor and flees, but it's the way the episode plays out that makes it so stellar.

Lorne's power to read minds through song has always been treated like a fun gag, but there are two moments in the whole series where it works for dramatic purposes, and both are blood-curdling. The second one will come in season five and features Fred singing You Are My Sunshine.

The first one is here, as Lorne overhears Wesley (holding baby Connor) hum a lullaby to hush the baby. That's all it took for Lorne to realize what was going down and Wesley, desperate to escape, attacks his friend to stop him from ruining his plans. It's one of those moment-of-truth / point-of-no-return moments that define a character, and it sets Wesley on the path he will never really recover from.

With Lorne out, Wesley escapes, carrying Connor with him. He doesn't far before his throat is slit by an associate of Holtz and the baby is stolen. This all happens in a single episode by the way, in case you forgot. On occasion, Angel's show was bananas in terms of how much plot it crammed into a single outing. In the end, a portal to a Hell Dimension is opened and Holtz and Connor go in, ending a whirlwind episode that leaves the viewer stunned and blown away.

It doesn't matter that the time-shifting Sahjhan manipulated the prophesy that convinced Wesley that Angel was a threat to Connor. It doesn't matter that the whole inciting incident that put Wesley on the path that ended with Connor being kidnapped twice-over was entirely a lie. Wesley made his choices and will live with the consequences. His throat was cut and he went to the hospital. The rest of the team sort of half-way forgave him, understanding that the was essentially lied to and tricked into what he did. After that, Angel pays him a visit, bringing this mini-arc to a booming (but ultimately unresolved) conclusion...

Angel is a very different show compared to Buffy. Its more serialized nature makes it hard to review the episodes one by one. Instead, it's better to consider them arc by arc, but even then that's a messy business because so many of the arcs overlap each other. Unlike Buffy, whose one-off episodes served as the backbone to the whole affair, Angel would have worked better with the kind of shorter, arc-heavy seasons that modern TV shows have on streaming services.

Looking back on the season, it's the big picture that stands out, and episodes like "Double or Nothing" (which sees Gunn have to deal with gambling debts), that come after so much intensity sort of killed the momentum. It's a credit to how well done those arcs were, though, that they elevate the whole season in spite of the filler that's sprinkled throughout.

The final trio of episodes brings us back to the main arc of the season, as Connor returns at the end of episode twenty, now looking like a teenage Pete Campbell. As with season two, the final handful of episodes serves as a teaser for what's to come in the next season. We learn very little about Connor at the end of season three but it's clear he's going to be a major part of the show going forward (or so we think).

In hindsight, it's easy to see how the creators were playing with fire trying to bring in another new character so deep into the show's run. It worked with Fred, but that was the exception. The overall backlash against Connor (most of which will be felt throughout season four) is more of the rule.

Still, at this point, we end season three only with good vibes. It also closes with a banger cliffhanger, as Holtz commits suicide via icepick, leaving his corpse with a pair of puncture wounds in his neck and leaving Connor to believe his blood father murdered the only man who has raised him in Hell for the past eighteen years. It's the final act of a man completely consumed by vengeance and it ends season three on a high note.

It seemed as though Angel had not only found its groove but was climbing higher faster than ever thought possible. As season three ended, the show was looking like the Star Trek DS9 of the franchise; the darker, more serialized, character-driven show that gets better and better every year. Unfortunately, creative decisions caused by internal and external problems will kill its momentum in season four and leave its future more uncertain than ever.

Chapter Nine

BUFFY SEASON SIX

uffy is dead. Wait no that's not right. How about: "Buffy **was** dead." No, that's not quite it either. Let's try this one: "Buffy died." Yes, that's fine. Let's start there. Buffy died and yet her show did not.

It's pretty ballsy to end a season with your main character leaping to her death as a heroic sacrifice to save the world. It's less ballsy when you're ending an entire series that way but even then it's a pretty bold move for a showrunner to make. In the former case, you're basically telling the audience "don't worry, this will all work itself out somehow," which runs the risk of rendering the emotional impact of the sacrifice completely neutered. In the latter case, you're basically telling the audience "this is it; the show is done and there is nothing more to say on the subject."

Star Trek DS9 ended with Ben Sisko's heroic sacrifice, but even that—the ballsiest and boldest of all the Trek shows—was done only half-heartedly, with the wink-and-nod assurance that he was still alive, in a sense, and could always come back some day.

Breaking Bad managed to pull it off with the death of Walter White, but that example only proves the point: Fans to this day continue to speculate and wonder if he's really dead, if the wound that finally put him down was fatal, etc. Nevermind the fact that Walter White was hardly a hero in the conventional sense.

Basically, unless there's a burial and a shot of a body in the casket (or at the very least a shot of a gravestone) as the screen fades to black, fans will always wonder and hope. The number of TV shows that ended with the absolute, definitive death of the main character is tremendously small.

As far as the WB was concerned, Buffy Summers died in the final episode of the fifth season. And, as far as the WB was concerned, the final episode of the fifth season was the final episode of the TV series entitled "Buffy the Vampire Slayer."

In the days leading up to the episode, "The Gift," commercials on the network and ads in the TV Guide billed it as "The WB Series Finale." It was an odd phrasing; nothing else was ever written in such a way. When Cheers ended, it wasn't called "the NBC Series Finale." When M*A*S*H ended it wasn't promoted as "the CBS Series Finale." So what gives?

Buffy was dead, but her show wasn't.

Already the deal was in place for UPN to continue the series, with a two-season contract that promised Joss Whedon something he had never been given before with the WB: Job Security. Finally, after season finale after season finale of having to write the year's final episode as a possible "final-final" episode, now he had the freedom to tell a longer story, spread out over two years.

This deal was not fully solidified when "The Gift" was written, however, which meant if the show was never picked up, season five's final episode would have to be its last. This was an all-or-nothing finale; either Buffy would end for good or it would continue on for a guaranteed two more seasons.

Instead of hedging his bets, Joss and co. ended year five in the most "final" way possible: Buffy dies, her friends mourn, the hero is buried, and her gravestone is the last thing we see as the screen fades to black. That was it. It was over. Buffy died.

Until, later that summer, ads started popping up and billboards started appearing, all bearing the same two words:

BUFFY LIVES

So begins year six of Buffy the Vampire Slayer, a season that has divided the fanbase more than any other. To put it simply, this is a messy year, filled with writing that is occasionally as weak as anything we've seen since season one, as well some decisions for the characters that, frankly, continue to anger fans to this day. And yet, in spite of its messiness, there is a beauty to this year, one which might not have been apparent in the original week-to-week episodic release, but which is made much more obvious when binge-watched years later.

In terms of ranking, while I will provide a full episode-by-episode "worst to best" analysis later, it's worth mentioning here that season six has only a single episode ranked in the top-eleven, tied with season one for the fewest. On the other hand, that single episode is (spoiler) the single greatest episode in the show's entire run. It also has the single worst episode in the entire "worst to best" ranking, with a disastrous hour that beats out even the loathsome "Beer Bad." Again, it's a messy season, full of extremes, but when viewed as a whole it has a lot to admire.

Perhaps the biggest criticism against the year is that it is the most brooding, dour, even occasionally "depressing" season of the series. On that point, I agree entirely. What I don't agree with, however, is the idea that it being depressing is a criticism. On the contrary, the season is about depression. That is the theme being explored. Remember...

Every Buffy season explores a key aspect of life and maturity befitting the title character's age and development. In season one, Buffy tackles her calling. In season two, it's her first love. In season three, it's the end of childhood. In season four, it's the awkward transition between being immature and mature. In season five, it's the grim realities of adulthood. In season six, it's depression and finding a reason to live.

The internal struggle this year, about dealing with depression and finding a reason to keep on living live again, is tackled, outwardly, through the challenges posed by the season's big bad. And who is this big bad? At first, you might think it's those nerdy goobers, dubbed "the trio" or "the losers." The threesome of Warren, Jonathan, and Andrew vow to make Buffy's life a miserable wreck for all the pain she had previously inflicted on them.

But while "the trio" do play Buffy's foil for most of the year, they are not the Big Bad of the season. You might think the real villain of the year is Willow, who goes dark for the final few episodes and tries to do the "big bad" thing that Buffy's Big Bads seemingly try to do every season: destroy the world. But again, that's not it. Well, technically that's almost it, but not quite. No, the real Big Bad of season six is the Scooby Gang.

Well, okay, to be fair, Tara and Dawn are completely innocent. The rest of them, though, in particular the core threesome that have been together from the beginning—Buffy, Willow, and Xander—are the real villains of the year.

Throughout the duration of Buffy's sixth year, our heroes give into their worst impulses and struggle in adulthood, as people without parents or guardians helping them frequently do. And though every Buffy season explores its main theme for the year both internally and externally, season six is the one year where those two ideas are as closely interwoven as they would ever be.

The real enemies of season six are the "personal demons" we all wrestle with as we try to figure out life in our 20s, and those personal demons make the lives of our characters miserable all season long.

Xander struggles breaking out of the long and ugly shadow of his deadbeat, alcoholic father, whose marriage is in shambles and whose life is spent mostly with him wasting away in a recliner with a beer in hand and a perpetual five o'clock shadow on his face. In what should be Xander's highest and greatest moment as a character—his wedding day—he faces his ultimate test: Will he solidify his character growth over the past six years, marry a woman he genuinely loves, and become the man he can be? Nope.

He cowers. He caves. He gives in to his worst fears. He runs away, leaving his bride at the altar, refusing to go through with his marriage simply because he can't shake the fear that he might become the same sort of deadbeat husband that his own father is. Do we hate watching Xander make such foolish and stupid and hurtful decisions? Yes.

After six years we have invested in the character and, after six years, Joss Whedon is allowed to make us feel shame and pity and frustration toward him. Life isn't always rainbows and happiness and always making good choices. It's much messier and Xander's actions this year remind us of that.

Willow struggles with her own persistent insecurities and negative feelings of her self-worth, something which she had been successfully repressing over the past few years as her magical powers blossomed. The problem is, Willow's insecurities never went away, and the more powerful she becomes as a witch, the more she comes to believe it's the only "good thing" about her that's of any value to anyone. That's a very dangerous personal philosophy to hold, and when her friends try to tell her that too much reliance on magic is becoming a problem, she shuts them down and shuts them out, growing darker and more isolated as a result.

Tara is there to try and keep Willow grounded but even she is shunned. Instead, she turns to Amy, the minorist of all minor characters, who returns in what, admittedly, is a killer bit of continuity commitment. Amy brings out all the worst impulses in Willow, leading to her becoming her most reckless and ugly self. When she finally crosses the line and nearly gets Dawn killed, she seems to revert, but really it's an insecure character retreating back to her insecurities.

Having already gotten a taste of what, to her, defeats those negative feelings, her respite from magic was never going to last. After Tara is killed, Dark Willow emerges and there is seemingly no pulling her back to the light.

MATTHEW L. MARTIN

From a writing standpoint, I rank the first part of the Dark Willow storyline among the worst-written and acted episodes of the whole series, but after binging the entire twenty-two-episode run, it's much more tolerable than it was back in 2001-2002. The worst of it only lasts for two episodes ("Smashed" and "Wrecked") and after that things improve instantly.

At the time, "Wrecked" was the last hour to air before the winter break, meaning no new episodes aired for five weeks; that's a long time to stew over what is, in my opinion, the single worst Buffy episode of them all. Today, however, the episode is over and the next one is on mere moments later.

Binging the season helps see the storyline as a single entity and appreciate what is going on with Willow's very damaged character this year. Of course, we didn't even mention one of the big catalysts for Willow's conflicting feelings this season is the knowledge that her (very dark and complicated) spell to bring Buffy back from the dead, did not—as Willow believed—rescue her from Hell, but actually pulled her out of Heaven.

Buffy's storyline this season is nothing short of tremendous, but that's an opinion hardly felt twenty years ago. Back then there was too much talk about the will they/won't they with Spike, the glum attitude she had for most of the year, and how miserable she seemed some of the time, while being overly chipper the next. It seemed like bad writing. It seemed unfocused and inconsistent. In fact, it was the best realization of the messiness of depression ever displayed in "genre TV."

Buffy begins the year in a coffin, ripped away from the afterlife by her friends, and then spends the next few episodes in a haze, trying and failing to "just get back to normal." It all comes to a head in the seminal episode "Once More With Feeling," where it is revealed to her friends that Buffy was happy where she was, having saved the world and given her life to do it. Now she's been forced away from all that and thrown back into the messy, ugly, wicked world all over again.

Not only does her sacrifice feel pointless (what changed? evil is still rampant), but the reward she was enjoying because of that sacrifice is taken away from her. No wonder she's depressed. And yet, all she hears from her friends is "suck it up and get over it" (not in so many words, but that's how she interprets their words and actions). Naturally she'll put on a lying face and smile for them when she can, and it makes perfect sense, too, that she would give in to her worst impulses and engage in a prolonged relationship with a soulless Spike.

MATTHEW L. MARTIN

What's most remarkable about this year is how the episode everyone loves from the season, "Once More With Feeling," is often lauded as being a happy oasis in a sea of gloominess. In reality, "Once More With Feeling" is the most poignant episode of the whole series. It might not be as straightforwardly sad as "The Body" but it's a close second. The difference is that it hides its sadness behind the song and dance numbers.

When you read the lyrics to the songs in question you soon realize that Joss used his "musical episode" as a way to sort of lay out his thesis for the whole season. I'll have a detailed write-up of the whole episode and all its numbers later, but for right now, just focus on the second verse of the big show-stopping song at the end:

Life's a song
You don't get to rehearse
And every single verse
Can make it that much worse

Still, my friends don't know why I ignore
The million things or more
I should be dancing for

All the joy, life sends
Family and friends
All the twists and bends
Knowing that it ends

BUFFY THE VAMPIRE SLAYER

Well, that depends
On if they let you go
On if they know enough to know
That when you've bowed
You leave the crowd

Buffy basically says that she knows all the things people love about life, and that she should be happy to sing about them, but she can't. She used to live that life, but then she died. That life was over but instead of letting her go, her friends intervened. She played her part, did her bow, and left, only to be forced back...

There was no pain
No fear, no doubt
'Till they pulled me out
Of Heaven
So that's my refrain
I live in Hell
'Cause I've been expelled
From Heaven
I think I was
In Heaven

So, give me something
to sing about
Please
Give me something

MATTHEW L. MARTIN

It's worth noting that the demonic curse that permeates the episode is the fact that singing and dancing is now life-threatening. If you don't stop, you will dance till you spontaneously combust...which is what Buffy starts to attempt when she asks for something (happy) to sing about.

When no answer is given, she starts dancing, and smoking, about to die. That's what she wants in the moment. That's what she wants this whole season: She wants something to sing about. She needs something to pull her out of her depression. Of course, it's Spike who stops her before she dies, and sings to tell her his own thesis...

Life's not a song
Life isn't bliss
Life is just this
It's living
You'll get along
The pain that you feel
You only can heal
By living
You have to go on living
So one of us is living

Ever the nihilist-poet, Spike basically tells Buffy there is no happy answer, only further existence. It's hardly what she needs in the moment, but it's something, and what will come from it is a sordid relationship built on Spike's "just live" philosophy. To say that road will lead both down to a dark place would be putting it mildly. Before the song ends, however, Dawn adds a final line, and it's a callback to something Buffy said to her just before she leapt to her heroic death...

The hardest thing in the world is to live in it.

What a fantastic callback this is. The first time we heard it came at the end of "The Gift," as Buffy decided she had to die a hero. Now we hear it after Buffy has resigned herself to die as a way to give up and succumb to her depression. Dawn's words are a sobering reminder that dying will not solve the problem this time as it did last time. Buffy walks away, not necessarily determined to live, but no longer prepared just to end it all right there.

Again, I'll have much more to say about "Once More With Feeling" at the end of the book. Before moving on, I want to leave this here...

DEPRESSION HOTLINE USA: 1-800-662-4357

DEPRESSION HOTLINE UK: +44 (0) 8457 90 90 90

MATTHEW L. MARTIN

So with "Once More With Feeling" establishing the thesis, not only with Buffy and her depression, but with Xander's lingering uncertainty regarding his wedding, and Willow's careless over-reliance on magic, the rest of the year explores just how much damage the core trio of Scoobies can do to themselves.

They're helped along the way by outside factors, of course; Halfrik prods Anya and Xander into doubting how right for each other they really are, Amy goads Willow into going deeper into dark magic, and Spike operates as a devil on Buffy's shoulder, encouraging her to give into her most self-destructive tendencies.

Everything comes to a head at different moments for the Scoobies. For Xander, his rock bottom comes in the episode "Hells Bells," where a version of himself from the future goes back in time to show him a premonition revealing how he will become exactly the kind of deadbeat he always feared. Even when he learns the "future Xander" was really just a demon out for revenge against Anya, Xander doesn't care; the vision—fake or not—hit too close to home. He runs away, sending Anya into her own dark place.

Why Xander? Why must you be so short-sighted? That's the question fans asked at the time, believing the writing was doing the character a disservice. Actually, it was perfectly in line with where the character was at that point in time. The fact is, he's a slave to his upbringing, as we all are to some extent. He loves Anya too much to subject her to be what he thinks a husband/father is (his own father). Running away from his responsibility, running away from the grown-up thing is the only thing that makes sense to him. He can't be the brave adult he needs to be, he thinks.

For Willow, she has not one but two rock bottom moments. First, when she's high on dark magic, she crashes a car and nearly kills Dawn. This happens not even halfway through the season (episodes nine and ten, "Smashed" and "Wrecked"), but just when we think she's turning the corner, a stray bullet ends the life of Tara, and Willow—who had been suppressing her temptations to use magic—unleashes everything she has, to the point where she tries to destroy the world.

Why Willow? Why must you be so entirely evil, so suddenly? That's the question fans asked at the time, believing the writing was doing the character a disservice. Actually, it was perfectly in line with where the character was at that point in time. She's not trying to destroy the world for some silly "she's evil and that's what evil people do" reason. She's not The Master (season one) or Angelus (season two). She wants the world to end because that's what she can do...and what she can't do is bring Tara back. She needs control. She lost control when she gave up magic and what happened was her loved one died in her arms. Control is all she has left, and in her pain and anger, using her control over the world to "end it all" is the only thing that makes sense to her. She has nothing left, she thinks.

For Buffy, her rock bottom comes about a dozen different times in a dozen different ways. I mean just pick one: There's her being forced to work at the Doublemeat Palace...which is topped by her ex-boyfriend Riley (blech) popping in to see her with his new wife in tow. There's the magical side-effect that a demon gives her, which causes her to believe that her entire life—being a Slayer, saving the world, etc—is just a figment of her mentally-broken imagination, and that the real Buffy Summers is in a mental institution. There's the other side-effect of a demon baddie that causes her to think she accidentally killed an innocent person. And there's the feeling of shame she feels over her ongoing tryst with Spike.

Buffy, Willow, and Xander all have it hard this year as they battle their own personal demons. And yet, as much as season six is about the heroes sinking into the pits of their worst impulses, the year does not end on a sad note. On the contrary, the finale is one of the most uplifting and hopeful of them all. In the end, all three overcome their personal demons and close the year on a positive note.

In the end, Xander rises to the occasion when it matters most. He might've withered at his wedding, but when the world was at stake, he stood up to Dark Willow and got through to the kind-hearted person that was buried under all that dark magic. He reached her in away no one else could, not even Buffy. Willow and Buffy had been friends since tenth grade; Xander and Willow had been friends since Kindergarten, and the "yellow crayon" speech he gives brings out the tears, not only in Willow but in everyone watching at home...

It's so darn cheesy. The special effects are shoe-string budgeted, the makeup and costuming is peak late-90's/early 00's (baggy...everything baggy, and goth!), but after six years of getting to know these characters...the scene just works. Buffy doesn't save the world this time. She did that last year. This time it's Xander who does it, because Xander was the only one who could.

In the end, Willow lets go and decides to cry and mourn for Tara rather than end the world over it. Seeing as how Tara was one of, if not the, purest, kindest, and most harmless characters in the series, that's exactly what she would have wanted. Willow embraces her friend and saves the world simply by deciding not to destroy it. That's maybe understating things, but

MATTHEW L. MARTIN

it's all right there in Xander's big moment; they overlap.

And in the end, Buffy—who began the year by climbing out of a grave—ends the year in much the same way. At the start of the season, she climbed out against her will, entering a dark and wicked world. At the end of the season, she climbs out with a renewed sense of purpose, and enters a bright and hope-filled world that awaits her.

Buffy's sixth's season is hardly the show's tightest, most focused, or highest-quality batch of episodes. What it offers, however, is a powerful analysis of how we—people, us—are often our own worst enemies, capable of hurting ourselves and our loved ones in a way no one else can. What we often need is some perspective, a reminder that we're loved, and someone to show us that life is still worth living, no matter what.

Oh and as for Spike? He has his own little character arc this year, the low point of which is an attempted rape of our main heroine. It's easily the most uncomfortable five minutes you'll have watching this TV show, and though I didn't like it (who would?), I can at least say it wasn't done for nothing. Spike—soulless vampire that he was—felt remorse and shame, something hard for a vampire to come by. In response, he left Sunnydale and ended up in the hut of a shaman who, after the obligatory trials and hardships were endured, granted him what he needed to, in his words "give Buffy what she had coming to her."

Spike restored his soul as the credits rolled.

Buffy's sixth season ended in a way no prior year did: It ended with a cliff-hanger. With the promise of another year already guaranteed, Joss kept us hanging, wondering what was coming next, in the show's seventh and final season.

MATTHEW L. MARTIN

Chapter Ten

ANGEL SEASON FOUR

Let's get right to it: Angel's fourth season is a hot mess. What it has in its favor is a cast that is completely in tune with their characters, a writing staff that knows how to write "moments" and a devil may care attitude that prevails over the whole affair. As I will say again, in the Buffy Season Seven summary...

> Creator Joss Whedon signed a two-season deal with the [UPN] network. Also, as part of the agreement, Joss was guaranteed that Angel would be moved

*over to UPN as well in the event of it being
canceled after its fourth season. A small
part of me believes Joss subconsciously
sabotaged Angel's fourth season in the
hopes WB would do exactly that.*

While I won't go so far as to seriously
entertain the notion that Joss intentionally
sandbagged one of his shows, I will allow myself
space to wonder if he didn't deliberately try to
toss a half-dozen different ideas out there
without rhyme or reason, to see what would
work, not worrying about the repercussions
because he knew he had a fallback should WB
decide to cancel the show. I'm not saying that
happened, certainly not that it happened
consciously, but subconsciously? Yeah, I can see
Joss thinking "let's try this and if it doesn't work,
we'll just eighty-six it. What are they gonna do,
cancel us?"

Very little about the overall picture of the
season works, and even though Angel had, by
this point, sort of settled into a formula where
every season was broken into thirds (big arc to
start, big arc in the middle, mini-arc that ends
the season with a cliffhanger), there were always
through-lines that gave the whole season a
cohesive feel. Not here.

There's an attempt, maybe, and on paper
you can make a case for it, but in execution it's

non-existent. In season four, there are multiple little arcs that begin and end abruptly, overlap each other, and offer little in the way of character development or payoff.

Other than one massive change to a core cast member, the first twenty-one episodes (of the twenty-two-episode season) keep everyone either entirely static or, in the case of Angelus' return, only temporarily changed. For a show that butters its bread on the development and evolution of its characters, it's worth noting that such evolution is viewed over the course of its entire five-year run, and in that run, season four is, for the most part, a year-long stretch where almost everyone spins in the mud.

I say almost because one character does go through some radical changes, and that's Cordelia. Unfortunately, the circumstances behind the scenes with actress Charisma Carpenter fueled the changes to the character Cordelia, and not for the better.

First of all, let's remember who we're talking about here: Charisma Carpenter's Cordy is an OG Buffy character. She's been there from the beginning. She was the original "human" villain of the show and slowly grew into an anti-hero and even a genuinely sympathetic hero character before moving over to Angel. The Cordy from Buffy Season One could never have worked as part of a core trio of characters on Angel, but after three years of steady growth and development, she had blossomed into the perfect comedic charmer that a series with such a dark and brooding leading man needed.

Throughout Angel's first three seasons, Cordy continued to develop, to the point where, by the end of season three she was a believable love interest for Angel, something no one—and I mean no one—would have bought when the series began. It's a credit to Joss and his writers in that they crafted the perfect "ill-fated lovers" duo in Buffy and Angel and somehow managed to create an additional love interest for each that you would never believe could work unless you saw it on screen.

And then Angel's third finale happened.

I didn't talk much about this in the previous Angel chapter, because I knew it fit better here: Basically the third season ends with a customary cliffhanger, but the focus of the episode's ending is on Angel being left to rot at the bottom of the ocean, and not on what happened to Cordelia, which is a shame because no one doubted for a second that Angel would fail to escape his confines and resume being the hero of the show. That presumption sort of spilled over, perhaps intentionally, into thoughts about the fate of Cordelia. Everyone assumed she'd be okay, but instead, she (spoiler alert) wasn't, and it hurt the fanbase of the show as a result.

So what happened to Cordelia? Well, at the end of season three she encounters Skip, who tells her she can do more good for Angel and co. by ascending to a higher plane of existence. Mind you this happens at the same time Angel is being tossed into the ocean by his vengeful son and surrogate vampire-hunter father.

That's a fun sentence.

The thrust of the final episode of season three is that Angel and Cordy are finally going to confess their feelings to each other. Except, before they can, they are, seemingly, separated forever. Of course, TV viewers know how cliffhangers work; there's no such thing as forever. Angel sinks to the ocean and Cordy ascends to a heavenly light above. We end the season knowing they'll get back together but unsure how.

Season Four begins with a mini-arc focused around bringing Cordelia back (Angel returns, as expected, right off the bat). When she does, she has amnesia, which is red flag number one for the season as amnesia storylines are always just the worst on TV. It does provide us a fun little Joss Whedon-directed one-off episode, "Spin the Bottle," in which everyone reverts (mentally) to their teenage selves. The arc ends there and immediately we're dealing with a demonic monster called "The Beast" that blocks out sunlight and wants to wreak havoc on everything. It soon becomes clear that The Beast is being controlled by someone and, shock of shocks, we discover it is Cordy of all people.

Well, the fan surmises, *clearly this isn't Cordy because she would never go evil like this. She's either being mind-controlled or this is an imposter of sorts.*

We're led to expect a grand reveal that will end with Cordy returning, the proper bad guy getting defeated, and everyone picking up the pieces together. Instead, we get another mini-arc that sees Angelus return in the most convoluted fashion, as well as the return of Faith, which serves more to reintroduce her to the world before he heads off to Buffy Season Seven.

Angelus' big comeback to the Buffyverse was a big deal at the time and WB marketed the heck out of it, but the end result is a far cry from the latter half of Buffy Season Two. There it felt like a natural progression of the story. Here it feels like a ratings stunt.

The whole thing ends with a kind of wet fart episode, as Angel and Angelus share the screen in the mind of the main character while guest star Willow restores his soul. I won't hate on Willow; on the contrary, Alyson Hannigan fits in with this cast like hand-in-glove and, had she joined the show for season five, it would have been magical. She's the lone bright spot in this otherwise dreary mini-arc.

The storylines shift again after Angel is back to normal, this time with everyone wanting to know why Cordy went bad. It turns out she is very very pregnant, and in a relationship with the much younger Conner, whose diapers she changed as a surrogate mother not one year ago. I don't care how you rationalize the time-shenanigans of being in a demon dimension, this was weird and creepy and I don't like it at all. The arc ends abruptly as Cordelia gives birth to a fully grown woman. This takes us all the way into left field for the final mini-arc of the season, centered around the villain Jasmine.

I should start by pointing out that there are moments in this arc that are very well done, especially the decision to make Fred the hero. The big picture idea of it is also great: Jasmine wants to bring peace on earth at the cost of a few people here and there that she will eat from time to time. What's a few people when you can stop all wars and violence? It's a great ethical question and the payoff is brilliant, but it's the little details that have to hold it all together, and they all fall flat.

But nevermind that, because really the show does nothing with this arc; the whole thing is wiped from everyone's memory by the last episode anyway. It doesn't matter. But while everyone is talking about Jasmine this and world peace that you know what we're not talking about? Cordelia! She basically drops off the map.

What we will learn in the next season, which 1 will spoil here because it's relevant, is that Cordelia is dead, and has been since the end of season three. Nothing we see in season four is really Cordelia. She's gone. Season Four Cordy is just a pale imitation whose only purpose is to bring Jasmine into the world...only to be discarded in time for Jasmine to be discarded before the season even ends.

So what on earth happened?

Charisma Carpenter got pregnant and the plans for season three had to be scrapped just before production began. In response, Joss and co. decided their new idea would be to write a story in which Charisma's character gets pregnant and gives birth to the villain of the season. Looking back, you can sort of see how the entire year is about Cordelia bringing Jasmine into the world and thus, in a meta way, how the whole season is Joss' angered expression of frustration over how much Carpenter getting pregnant messed things up.

Apparently working her pregnancy into the show in a normal way wasn't possible, despite the fact that they have literally made the character pregnant before on the show. Instead, the story they settled on was to turn Cordelia into a villain and then retroactively have her be dead going back to the end of season three. It feels like a slap in the face to a character who helped define this series and was a bright spot for the show in its very rocky early episodes.

Cordy's growth from "vapid high school mean girl" to "essential cog in the Angel Investigations wheel" is one of the best evolutions of a character in the whole Buffyverse. For it to end with such a deliberate whimper is more than unfortunate; it's shameful.

Angel's fourth season ends with a last episode akin to Buffy Season Four's "Restless," in that it comes after the big bad is defeated and the arc is ended, and deals with the fallout. As the heroes are told, by defeating Jasmine, Angel and his team essentially stopped world peace. That makes them, in the eyes of the ever-villainous Wolfram & Hart, the worst bad guys in the history of the world. Naturally, Angel is offered the chance to go pro with his evilness, and take over the law offices to do with as he pleases. It's a really clever little twist and one that almost makes the slog of the season that preceded it worthwhile. But, as with the season as a whole, it's not the idea but the execution that falters.

Angel's condition to take over the Office is that essentially the past two years be erased from everyone's memory. That means Conner, Cordy, Jasmine, Wesley going bad, getting betrayed, turning bitter; it's all wiped from the record books with the team starting over from scratch.

If there's a more audacious reboot of a series this deep into its run (that works as well as it will) I haven't seen it. But then again, these are the same people who introduced Dawn on Buffy's show in a way that avoided all the tropes and cliches typical to a "new character comes into a show late in its run" shakeup. It's not a surprise that they would try it here and, as said, it pays off. Though, sadly, not enough to save the show for more than a single extra season.

MATTHEW L. MARTIN

Chapter Eleven

BUFFY SEASON SEVEN

Throughout the summer of 2001, UPN aggressively marketed the upcoming sixth season of Buffy the Vampire Slayer, focusing on an ad campaign that featured only two words: "Buffy lives."

As we noted in the previous chapter, the move brought some changes to the show, with the biggest being the fact that creator Joss Whedon signed a two-season deal with the network. Also, as part of the agreement, Joss was guaranteed that Angel would be moved over to UPN as well in the event of it being canceled after its fourth season. A small part of me believes Joss subconsciously sabotaged Angel's fourth season in the hopes WB would do exactly that, but we'll get into the mess that was Angel Season Four later. Right now it's about Buffy Season Seven and, as said, this was the first time Joss was guaranteed another year on the air before work began on the current season. That allowed him to do something he had not done with the previous five finales of Buffy; he gave us a cliffhanger.

Season six ended with Spike getting a soul.

That's it. There's no big villain reveal, no cataclysmic danger left unresolved. Basically, all the loose threads in season six were tied up except for one, but since the show had devoted so much writing and focus on Spike (on account of his being so beloved by audiences and so much fun to write for), the promise of more to come was enough to help gin up a sizeable bit of interest in season seven. The bigger selling point, though, was the promise that this would be Buffy's final year.

Seven years feels right, but maybe that's because I grew up with Star Trek: TNG, DS9, and Voyager, which all got seven seasons before bowing out. It might've felt odd to other fans, however, since the show had only just made a big deal out of Buffy's death with the very "series finale-feeling" ending to season five.

The announcement that season seven would end show instantly made seasons six and seven feel like an extended coda and, in fact, that's a common assessment that is still held by fans today. For many, Buffy did end with season five's "The Gift." Everything after was either a very good, very messy, or very bad epilogue, depending on your personal preferences.

For me, I rate the UPN years somewhere in between "very good" and "very messy." These last two seasons are certainly not perfect, but there's a lot to love here, whether in the big picture/thematic sense in season six or in the individual moments sprinkled throughout season seven.

Every Buffy season is almost always remembered in conjunction with the Big Bad that dominates the year. In season one it was The Master, in season two it was Spike...until it was Angelus. In season three it was The Mayor. In season four it was the Initiative. In season five it was Glory. In season six it was the personal demons and failings of the Scoobies themselves. With this being the final year, it's expected there would be a villain not only befitting the big ending, but also formidable enough to provide a showdown befitting the final finale.

To this point, Buffy (the show) has had several huge "final boss fight" moments in her finales, and all have had big dramatic stakes and poignant moments that lingered into future episodes. In season one's finale, Buffy died in her fight with the Master. The PTSD that short-lived death sparked carried over into the season two premiere. Season two ended with Buffy killing Angel to save the world.

Again, the heartbreak of that decision lasted into the third season. Season three ended with the school blowing up, the mayor being killed, and everyone saving the day...and then several of them leaving town after graduation; naturally season four features the people who were still around trying to figure out the brand new world they've been thrust into.

Season four might not end with a huge, climactic fight, but the many dreams found in the finale episode "Restless" are peppered with prophesies of things to come in the next season. Season five ends with Buffy dying. Not to be blunt about it but obviously, the consequences linger into season six; it goes without saying.

Season six ended, not with a whiz-bang fight, but with Dark Willow almost ending the world only to be talked off the ledge by her platonic soul mate. It's fitting, then, that season seven would begin with Willow still coming to terms, not only with the horror she wrought but with the power she was able to wield in the process. It's a seed planted—reminding us that it is Willow, not just the Dark version of her, exclusively, who possesses more power than anyone else in the show—that seems to go nowhere at first but which will pay off in spades at the end of the season.

As said, Willow isn't the only character whose arc gets delightful closure this season. The same is true of Spike and his newfound soul. The show wastes no time showing us the aftermath of his restored humanity and it's not pretty. The instant comparison viewers will want to make is to Angel, but it doesn't really work.

When we first meet Angel, he has been souled for a long time and has long since come to terms with it. He's still racked with guilt (a character trait that never really goes away) but he treats the guilt as part and parcel with the curse the gypsies put on him and is more than comfortable living with it. Spike, on the other hand, sought out his soul. He wanted it, and once he gets it—based on the rules of the Whedon universe—he gets the "lingering conscience" that comes with it.

Whereas Angel lives off a steady drip of guilt constantly flowing through his veins, Spike receives an instant defibrillator's worth of guilt and turmoil. The weight of it almost breaks him.

And while the character himself remains a bit polarizing among fans, for my money he's one of the most fascinating characters in the whole Whedonverse.

Here's what's amazing about Spike: Take away his soul and he's capable of terrible evil. Yes. That much is demonstrated repeatedly both during the series and especially in flashbacks. On the other hand, even without his soul, we see that Spike is equally as capable of kindness, warmth, humor, and even mercy. We see all that in the years before he regains his soul, an action which he only undertakes because he feels guilt over his attempted rape of Buffy, and because, in his own words in the second episode of season seven, he wanted to be the kind of man who would never do that.

Now contrast that with Angel, who does nothing but remorseless, merciless evil when he's without his soul, and who only got his soul put back in him because of a curse, and who actively worked to prevent Jenny from restoring it in season two's "Passion." Angel is presented as a Jekyll and Hyde character and, if anything, there are hints that Angel (the good side) is perfectly capable of stooping to the kind of evil that Angelus committed (we see that in season two of his show when he allows vampires to kill several members of Wolfram & Hart).

Spike, on the other hand, is not a dual-identity character; he's a single entity that moves between different polar extremes on his own personal spectrum. That's why he's such an incredible character. He has depth and layers that no other vampire on either show ever demonstrated.

The attempted rape is, let's be honest, such a black mark on his character that even talking about it in casual terms feels sleazy. It's certainly not easy to discuss it within the context of redemption, but the show demands it so let's give it that consideration.

In the Whedonverse, the soul is more than just a conscience. As already discussed, Spike demonstrates a conscience before he gains back his soul. Furthermore, it's not fair to say the soul in the Whedonverse is what gives people the ability to know right from wrong because, as we've seen, vampires know they're doing wrong, they just don't care, and even souled-people will do wrong and feel nothing about it.

It's no coincidence, I think, that in the same episode ("Seeing Red") that features Spike trying to rape Buffy (reminding those of us who maybe had forgotten that he is still a soulless half-demon), the "ordinary human" Warren also attempts to murder Buffy and inadvertently kills Tara. Even earlier in the season he clubs a girl in the back of the head and kills her (and then proceeds to try to cover it up). These are the actions of a souled-human and they are just as despicable as those committed by Spike or Angelus. Joss is telling us that the soul is not what makes a person good, nor is it just the conscience that tells people the difference between right and wrong.

So what is it, then?

I think the soul in the Whedonverse is what gives a person lingering, compounding feelings of guilt as a result of their bad actions. A vampire-like Spike might feel bad about a wrong he did: He demonstrates that in "Seeing Red" when he leaves Sunnydale to make things right. Furthermore, having a soul is stated in canon as the reason why Angel is so constantly burdened with guilt and why Spike is so instantly overwhelmed with it.

Putting it together, I think not having a soul in the Whedonverse means you might (but not necessarily) feel bad or remorse/guilt over a misdeed but the feeling doesn't linger; it fades like a passing thought because it takes "humanity" to feel genuine (persistent, nagging) guilt over those misdeeds, and the more misdeeds you do that are not rectified, the more that guilt weighs on you, with every crime becoming a rock you add to the pile you're forced to carry.

Being a vampire means sometimes you feel the weight of one rock, one crime, one heinous act but, in time, you just toss the rock down and go about your business without a care in the world. Spike, had he not set himself on a mission to change, might've found the feeling of guilt he had, immediately following the attempted rape, fade to a distant memory.

Instead, knowing that about himself, and knowing he didn't want that, Spike went on a quest to gain the missing thing that would restore his humanity; the thing that would make him suffer the lingering sting of guilt and, as a result, give him the motivation to be a decent person possessing "humanity."

Spike's arc ends perfectly this season, with him well and truly getting to play the hero and save the day, but it never would have happened had the show not allowed him to go on the journey it did. He went from being the evil bad guy in season two to chaotic neutral in season four to sympathetic anti-hero in season five, to a mirror/conduit for all of Buffy's worst impulses in season six, to, finally, a decent person who, at first is overwhelmed by all the wrong he did, and then decides to do something good for a change, not to undo the bad, but simply because it finally feels right to do it. What an amazingly written and performed character he was.

Spike isn't the only hero of the season, of course; this is still Buffy's show, though, during the season's worst moments, the show tends to forget about that. Let's remember...

Every Buffy season explores a key aspect of life and maturity befitting the title character's age and development. In season one, Buffy tackles her calling. In season two, it's her first love. In season three, it's the end of childhood. In season four, it's the awkward transition between being immature and mature. In season five, it's the grim realities of adulthood. In season six, it's depression and finding a reason to live. The final season is about letting go and moving into adulthood for good.

How does that play out this season? Who is the big bad that personifies that human struggle to move into adulthood? Well, in the context of Buffy, moving into adulthood means no longer carrying the burden of being "the" slayer. How that plays out is with the "potentials," the girls who are human lottery picks, any one of which could be magically endowed with all the powers of the Slayer in the event of Buffy's death. The big bad this year is trying to hunt them down and end the line of slayers for good. Who is it?

MATTHEW L. MARTIN

Curiously, it's a villain we met way back in season three's "Amends." In that episode, Angel was coming to grips with all the evil he committed during his season two rampage. Working against him was a non-corporeal manifestation of evil itself, called "the First." Essentially it is the manifestation of all evil everywhere. Being disembodied, it can neither hurt nor be hurt, but it is a master manipulator and capable of taking the form of any dead person, which it uses to taunt and prod people into committing destructive acts.

Throughout the final season the First takes many forms, most commonly that of Buffy herself (since she died in season one), but also Warren in order to manipulate Jonathan, as well as dead members of the potentials once Buffy starts sheltering them.

It's maybe a hair disappointing that a show subtitled "The Vampire Slayer" doesn't face off against a vampire as the final big bad, but by this point in the show vamps had become easily disposable fodder, no more threatening than Putties on Power Rangers.

Still, we're at least introduced to the übervamp, a particularly gnarly and superpowered version of the monster, which not coincidentally looks very similar to the "Grr Argh" monster that appears at the end of every credit roll. And in the final battle, we do face off against a horde of them, but the evil at the heart of the season is not a vampire but merely a philosophical representation of the whole concept of evil itself... which, now that I write that, is actually a pretty good idea.

One of the hardest lessons about moving to adulthood and fully leaving childhood behind is the grim reality that the problems you're soon to face are going to be there forever. Growing up the challenges we deal with change every couple of years as we develop and mature.

We go from dealing with wet diapers to nightmares to the first day of school to being bullied to hormones and puberty to the fear of leaving home and setting out; every few years it's a totally different mountain to climb and then one day, boom, you're an adult and forevermore it's your 9-to-5 job, managing your health, paying taxes, the rising cost of cereal, etc.

Not to get too depressing here but I can see how Joss might go from the crippling and perpetually crushing harsh realities of life and decide "the big bad to best represent that is the literal manifestation of all evil!"

How do you defeat "evil" itself? You don't. You can't. It's always going to be here as long as the world is spinning. Buffy's final shot is a triumphant one, with the heroine smiling after being asked what she's going to do next. She's smiling not because "evil" is destroyed. She's smiling because she's grown beyond having to fight evil's many forms all the time (I know in the comics she keeps fighting, but whatever). She's no longer the one and only end-all/be-all hero of humanity.

Evil isn't destroyed but in her last big battle, she stopped evil from winning, and now is happy to pass the torch onto the countless other potential slayers, whose powers are awakened, for them to fight evil wherever and however it may appear.

And how was such a victory pulled off? How were the potentials all able to take the power of the slayer?

Willow goes full Super Saiyan.

Perhaps my favorite thing about season seven is how it brings so much closure to everyone's character journey...except for Xander who doesn't have anything by way of an arc (losing an eye is not character development), and only kind of floats around running errands and occasionally offering sage wisdom (which I guess is his thing now). The stars of the season are Buffy, Spike, and Willow.

Willow's character begins season seven unsure how to move forward. She hit rock bottom in season six (as did everyone) and tried to fix the problem with her magic by quitting it cold turkey. That didn't work and only led to the explosion of evil in the final arc of the season.

Willow begins season seven trying to come to terms with the fact that she's become, perhaps, too powerful for her own good. As the year progresses, she's seen acting like the pensive, unconfident, meek Willow she was at the beginning of the series. It takes the new character/potential Kennedy to bring her out of her shell, and though Kennedy was not (and still isn't) a fan favorite, she serves that important storyline purpose. It maybe could have been written better in the finer details, and the acting could be a bit sketchy at times, but the idea is there and it's a good one.

That's a recurring theme this year: The big picture idea is a good one, but the finer points aren't always handled with care.

Season seven can best be divided into three parts. The first third of the year, constituting the season's first seven episodes, offers a lot of the one-off fun, Scoobie-like hijinks, and throwback charm that was missing for a lot of season six.

There are moments here that rival the absolute joy of the one-offs from seasons three and four. The episode "Him," for example, which features a love spell gone awry, offers what might be the second-greatest silent gag in the series (second only to Giles and the wizard costume), as Buffy (under the spell) decides the only way to prove her love for the man in question is to blow up Principal Wood with a bazooka.

The second chunk of the season (episodes eight through seventeen) is the largest of the three, and the messiest. To its credit, I will say that this stretch of episodes works remarkably better when binge-watched, something that also proves true when rewatching season six. Back in the day, having to go through these one by one, a week (or more) at a time, was agony, as many of these episodes were highly serialized, without any proper beginning or ending, and little in the way of theme or three-act structure to each outing.

The worst offenders of this are the pair of episodes "Bring on the Night" and "Showtime," in which Buffy first fights, and then kills her first übervamp. The plot that is spread thinly over these two episodes would have been better served within a single forty-five-minute runtime. There's a kind of meandering and padding in these two that makes it feel like the worst of Angel's fourth season. I remember a lot of grief about them too, much of which was due to there being a huge three-week gap in between.

There was a buzz going around that the season was unfocused and lacked a strong arc. I think a lot of the angst was because everyone knew this was the last season and people had expectations of it being something "more special" than the rest, when the fact is, it was always going to be a relatively normal Buffy season, at least in terms of its format.

The middle of the season spends its time putting the pieces in place to go warp-speed to the finale, while still finding time to have more great one-off episodes that give a last little spotlight to the show's lesser characters. "Potential" serves as our last proper "Dawn" focused episode, and it really highlights how far the character has come since her debut two years back.

"Storyteller" brings great closure to a character that the writers clearly fell in love with this year, Andrew. And "Lies My Parents Told Me" gives us more backstory on the seemingly bottomless well of backstory that is Spike. I didn't even mention the episode that ended the first third of the season, "Conversations with Dead People," which won the Hugo Award (every nerd's Oscar).

I've said in previous chapters how Buffy wouldn't have been Buffy without these great one-off episodes, which are basically a lost art in the 8-10 episode seasons of today's streaming world. The big picture arc of season seven doesn't kick into high gear until episode eighteen, and the set-up, which was sprinkled across seventeen prior episodes, probably could have been condensed to two or three without much lost along the way.

What would have been lost are the viewers' final chances to watch these characters we've grown to love cut loose, have fun, chew scenery, and just be themselves without the burdens of the season's arc weighing everything down all the time.

All the same, the big arc of the season rounds the final corner in episode eighteen with the introduction of Caleb. Played by the ever-delightful Nathan Fillion, Caleb provides a physical presence to operate on behalf of the formless "The First." Caleb can hit, stab, slap, jab, even poke an eye out, and ultimately, he can take a magic axe to the gonads in the name of girl-power. Also, Faith is back, which only reinforces the "tying up loose ends" feeling of the final season.

Unfortunately, while the middle of the season is the messiest, the end of the season is the most frustrating. With only five episodes to go, it's more than a little disappointing that so much time is devoted to the idea that Buffy is a bad leader and that somehow Faith is the one who should be in charge of the potentials. They try to hang the lampshade with Faith herself declaring that she's not leadership material, and she's right, but that line feels hollow when everyone from Dawn, to Willow(!), Giles(!!), and even Xander(!!!) all agree that Buffy should leave the house (**her** house by the way) while Faith takes over the group.

I'm sure there's a way to make this all work as a story-point, but the way they go about it, especially in how immediately hostile everyone is toward Buffy, just never clicks. The only saving grace in it all is that it makes Spike the ultimate hero, friend, and loyalist. He goes looking for Buffy, finds her, and then gives her the queen mother of all motivational speeches...

The moment leads to the two of them sharing a bed in a platonic way, bringing their insane "love" some much-needed closure. The issue of Buffy/Spike, especially when compared to Buffy/Angel will forever be a point of contention among fans of the series. For me, the Buffy/Angel relationship was about a sixteen-year-old girl being smitten by a brooding, mysterious guy with a dark past.

Angel's curse meant that they could never be together, which gave it a tragic Romeo & Juliet vibe that Whedon and co. knew exactly how to play (the climactic scene in season two's "I Only Have Eyes For You" is basically the meta-commentary on this). The more she couldn't have him, the more she wanted him, and vice/versa.

MATTHEW L. MARTIN

With Spike, the relationship was different. At times it was raw, abusive, toxic, even flat out "wrong," but unlike with Angel, Buffy knew who and what Spike was from the outset. She didn't know Angel's secret until she had already gone head over heels for him, and she didn't know the particulars of the curse until it was literally too late.

With Spike, Buffy saw him at his worst, hated him for it, and still fell for him all the same. In the final minutes of the final episode, she tells him she loves him, and even though he doesn't believe it, and even if she doesn't believe it, I believed it. Not all the time, but here and there, fading in and out over the course of multiple seasons, Buffy and Spike loved each other.

They're "twin flames" in my opinion.

After Buffy and Spike get closure on their relationship, there are basically no other pieces to set on the board. The final two episodes serve as the set-up and pay-off to the series finale.

In the set-up, the episode "End of Days," Buffy acquires the magic scythe needed to take Caleb out. It also leads to her learning the origin of the Slayer line, which began as some African shaman...or should I say sha-MEN, give demonic power to a girl to have her fight the forces of evil on their behalf. It's a little rapey and the show points that out and doesn't shy away from it, so good for them for not handwaving it all.

The big finale, fittingly, takes place at Sunnydale High, where hordes of übervamps are preparing to burst out of the Hellmouth underneath and consume the world. Buffy's plan? Go in there and stop them. It sounds like a suicide mission, especially since the dozen or so girls she has with her can barely fight a punching bag. That's where Willow comes in.

Willow's arc reaches its payoff as she unleashes all her power to become, not Dark Willow, but Light Willow, drawing from the power of the scythe to imbue every potential Slayer with Buffy's power, no longer limiting it to the "one-per person, deliverable upon the death of the former" loophole the Shamans imposed (probably because they didn't want an army of superpowered girls conquering them).

The army of slayers beat back the army of übervamps but more and more keep coming, leading to Spike saving the day at the cost of his life. The Hellmouth closes (though "there's another one in Cleveland," Giles reminds us helpfully), the world is saved, and everyone wonders what they will do next. The question goes to Buffy, who has no answer other than a relieved smile that, whatever she chooses, she knows she can make it without the weight of the world solely on her shoulders.

It's easy to compare season five's finale with the end of season seven. Joss himself noted, as he sat down to write the final episode of the series, that he felt more pressure than ever because, as he says, he had already written the perfect sendoff for the character and the show, and that was season five's last episode.

Instead of trying to top "The Gift," which would have been impossible, and instead of just settling for a retread, which would have been a big misfire, Whedon simply pivoted and presented a different kind of finale, one that eschews poignancy for closure.

I'll have more to say in my episode-by-episode ranking, but while Chosen is not ranked in the top ten outings of the show, it does come close, and it is—under the circumstances, being so close to the sublime season five finale—a beautiful ending, sufficiently capping off the arc of the season, ably wrapping up the two-season coda that began with the move to UPN.

And though it doesn't hit the heights of being the "perfect finale to Buffy" that season five's "The Gift" was, it is the actual finale, and as it is, "Chosen" was a fitting finale to a TV series about a single girl chosen to fight alone, who survived far longer than any Slayer should purely because she refused to fight alone; she broke the rules and included her friends along the way. And then, when the evil became so big and so overwhelming that "evil itself" was the big bad to stop, Buffy broke the rules again and empowered every girl everywhere with the ability and the strength to fight back, to take control, and as the show says, to "slay."

A fitting end to one of genre TV's best ever.

MATTHEW L. MARTIN

Chapter Twelve

ANGEL SEASON FIVE

Buffy is done, but the Buffyverse is not, and while the show that started it all might have finished its big storyline in a satisfying, poignant, and closure-bringing way, the torch was immediately passed to the other show, Angel, to bring an end to the entire television universe.

Considering the troubles Angel's third season (to a lesser extent) and fourth season (in a big way) had, a viewer might be forgiven to think the final season of Joss Whedon's TV world would fail to stick the landing.

You'd be wrong.

BUFFY THE VAMPIRE SLAYER

Angel's season five is many things all at once, many of them contradictory, and yet the end result is a magical year of television. On the one hand, it's a triumphant return to form for writer/director/creator Joss Whedon, whose final two seasons of Buffy were hit and miss, and his workload was spread thinly between multiple projects.

As Buffy drew to a close, so too did Angel's fourth season. As ever, the WB network held the show hostage, keeping the idea of a fifth season renewal an uncertainty until the last minute. When they did finally agree to finance a fifth year, they did so with several demands.

First, Joss Whedon would have to be the showrunner. To understand this in TV terms, think of the showrunner as the most hands-on, day-to-day creative force on a TV show. It's a position second only to the executive producer. If you're a Star Trek fan, think of the dynamic at work during Deep Space Nine's seven-year run.

Ira Steven Behr was the DS9 showrunner, starting with the third season. He oversaw the writer's room, laid out the big picture idea for each season, and did a pass over every teleplay to ensure a unified, consistent "voice" was followed in each episode. Behr was truly the driving force behind every bold risk that DS9 took and his writers (Ronald D. Moore, Rene Echevarria, Robert Hewitt Wolfe, etc) followed his lead in crafting their episodes. But at the end of the day, it was Rick Berman who had ultimate veto power. Case in point: When Behr wanted a year-long arc that covered a Dominion takeover of the station, it was Berman who ordered it cut down to a few episodes to open the season.

Back to Buffy/Angel: Joss Whedon was the showrunner for Buffy. He oversaw the writer's room, laid out the big picture idea for each season, and did a pass over every teleplay to ensure a unified, consistent "voice" was followed in each episode.

There are more than a few interviews by Buffy writers who freely admit that "if there's a killer line or hilarious quip, it was probably something Joss added at the last minute." He was not only showrunner but he was also executive producer, meaning Buffy was in almost every way his vision brought to life. The limited budget he had to work with and the demands of the network/censors were the only hurdles he regularly had to contend with.

For the first four seasons of Angel, Joss Whedon operated as executive producer, while David Greenwalt (seasons 1-3) and Jeffrey Bell (season 4) served as his showrunners. Joss was still heavily involved in the stories and big picture goings-on of the show (not to mention writing/directing several episodes), but he left it to his showrunners to guide things while he worked closely on Buffy (and Fray, and Firefly, and Serenity, and a run on the Astonishing X-Men comic).

With season five, the WB wanted a Joss Whedon at his most attentive and they got it. There's a feeling this year that Angel has not had before, and while you can also credit that to the other changes that were made to the show, you can't deny the ever-present Whedoniness of it all. For the first time since the show began, Angel felt like a Joss Whedon series, albeit one that didn't entirely lose the core identity it had developed along the way.

Second, the show would have to be more episodic. Easily the most obvious change to Angel this year vs. the previous is the fact that the big, multi-episode arcs that defined the show going back to its second (and arguably best) season had to be nixed in favor of more one-off episodes.

On the one hand, Buffyverse fans pointed the finger to the more serialized nature of Buffy's sixth and seventh seasons (especially the second half of season seven), and how it was not as well-received as past seasons were, as the reason behind the change. I, on the other hand, think it's more likely the WB executives saw the struggles Angel season four had in the ratings. The previous year had been the first to average under four million per episode and the storyline arc did little to build momentum for a new season.

While it's possible the network was partially influenced by Buffy's last two years being regarded as lesser compared to season five, I think it's more the case that WB wanted to course-correct and do something that would make the show more approachable to nonviewers who might catch a commercial the night before an episode aired. Once again, Whedon acquiesced to the studio's demands, and crafted twenty-two strong, individual plots, leaving the overarching stuff to the background, woven throughout each episode.

And you know what, I have to say, as much as I love a good Angel arc, I adore the "short story" style format that season five leans into. This is the first year where the individual episodes stand out. There's the one with the Lucha Libre mailman. There's the one with the puppets. There's the one about Harmony. There's the one with Cordelia. There's "A Hole in the World," an episode so stellar and gut-wrenching I remember the title and not just the plot.

Finally, the budget was going to take a serious hit. Neither Angel nor Buffy had much of a budget anyway. TV budgets in those days were already hilariously small compared to movies, even for the big Networks and their top shows. Today, top-tier TV shows attract monster budgets and have special effects comparable to major motion pictures.

You only need to compare the budget for a show like Lois and Clark in the mid-90s to the new Superman & Lois show on the CW. Sure, the latter show can benefit from better technology, but the effects on the newer show are comparable to those seen in a typical comic book movie, whereas the effects on the 90's show were laughable when compared to the effects work done in movies of the time.

And yet, even in that handicapped budgetary environment, Buffy and Angel still managed to have an even worse budget. Quite frankly it's astounding how much Joss and co. were able to squeeze out of the spare change they had to work with. It's a good thing they had amazing writers and characters you could easily identify with and connect to. If these shows had to get by on their looks they never would have made it past the first episode.

All that said, the WB had the audacity to take the already tight budget of Angel and slash it even more for the fifth season. To be fair, Angel was an expensive show for a network as little-watched as the WB was in those days.

On the other hand, Angel was in the top ten for network viewership every year and needed a much smaller budget than the newest hit for the channel, Smallville. The WB had shown a willingness to spend money on shows that needed a budget and which could appeal to an ad-friendly ratings demo. Angel had four years to prove it could do that and it did prove it year after year. Cutting its budget in year five felt like a shortsighted move to squeeze the last bit of life out of the show before canceling.

With a reduced budget, a need for episodic storytelling, and a showrunner ready to put his most impactful mark on the show, Angel entered its fifth season ready to embrace a big shakeup.

We had hints of what was to come at the end of season four which, in hindsight, almost feels like a Whedon pitch to the network for a way to get the show renewed. Instead of a dark, brooding series about a ragtag bunch of crimefighters battling demons both external and personal, Angel shifted gears to being about a bunch of pampered adults being given the keys to a multi-million dollar operation. The only catch is their new boss is evil incarnate, meaning the team will have to wrestle with the moral and ethical quandaries of working for an evil law firm (but I repeat myself) while trying to use the resources of said firm to fight the very evil that currently employs them.

On paper, it's a pretzel's worth of twists and knots and confusions, but on the screen, it works. As always, credit must go to head writer

Joss Whedon, who never slows the pace down long enough for you to wrap your head around the conflicts of interest running amuck here, and only ever slows down to zoom in—way past those confusing parts—to focus on the personal struggles that come with being a hero but working for a villain.

For the past several chapters of this book, I have repeated the fact that every season of Buffy tackled some aspect of "growing up."

Whether it's about understanding and accepting who you are (season one), dealing with the heartbreak of your first love (season two), graduating high school (season three), the messy confusing time that is being a freshman in college (season four), losing a parent and learning how to be an adult without a safety blanket (season five), grappling with the depression that comes with feeling like a failure as an adult (season six), or finally stepping out of adolescence and admitting that, while you don't have all the answers, you at least have the perspective to know the world is going to keep spinning without you trying to hold it up (season seven).

Angel never quite worked the same way. If anything, Angel was not about a handful of big lessons, but instead, was about one big lesson.

There's a line that is uttered early in season one that Joss has said he viewed as the thesis for the show: "If nothing we do matters then all that matters is what we do." In other words, it would be easy to be a defeatist, considering how evil the world is (and getting worse every day) but just because everyone else is evil doesn't mean we have to be. We can choose to be good, to do good, to buck the trend, to push against the tide.

It might end with the tide finally overwhelming us but so be it, at least we'll have done what we could. At no time is that idea challenged more than in Angel's final year, where his takeover of the evil L.A. branch of Wolfram & Hart means the temptation to compromise is more readily available than ever before.

Evil so surrounds Angel that he ends up working *for* evil, to the disgust of Buffy. If you want to find an allegory, there it is: Angel is a show about leaving high school and struggling as a start-up entrepreneur (season one), dealing with the drama that comes with bringing your personal life to work (season two), having a fallout with the coworkers you had come to view as a quasi-family (season three), completely losing your way for a bit as you struggle to keep your business afloat (season four), and then finally selling out to The Man and seemingly sacrificing your principles to "win" at life (season five).

The new episodic nature of the show perfectly complimented the shift to the law firm.

New clients meant a new story every week, and the addition of Spike to the roster (another one of WB's demands, apparently) meant new comedy and drama dynamics as well.

But as much as I loved watching each new plot unfold every week, I most appreciated how Joss and co. stuck to their guns and didn't forget that this show is about the people in the center, not any recurring guest of the week. Angel has always been about Angel and his struggle being an "evil monster" living in an evil world while trying to be a good person. Season five puts a spotlight on that and forces Angel to come to terms with his place in the world as a hero and as a potential figure of prophecy (the so-called chosen one who will fight for good in the final battle of the something something Shanshu).

In terms of stand-out episodes this year, three, in particular, come to mind. The first is "Smile Time," also known as "the puppet one." This is arguably the best one-off episode Angel ever did, though I say that while acknowledging its polarizing status among the fanbase. Some Angel fans rejected this episode outright, arguing it was stupid, silly, pointless, or worse, unfunny. For me, I thought it was one of the best "one-off" episodes in the Buffyverse and maybe the only one in Angel's library that could compete with those classic episodes from Buffy.

The other show was always great about having some special gimmick or concept with its one-off episodes, using the gimmick to advance the story forward in big ways. Think of how much plot progression we got in "Once More with Feeling" or how the relationship with Buffy and Riley took a big turn in "Hush."

Angel had already done a few of those kinds of episodes but never as big or bold as this. I can see why some Angel fans, who favored the more serious and brooding take on the show, might've been turned off by it all, but for my money watching Spike vs Puppet Angel makes my sides ache from laughter. Puppet Angel "vamping out" is somehow even better. And, in keeping with the tradition, the episode wasn't just a gimmick for the sake of it, but it used the circumstances as a way to process the Fred and Wesley storyline.

And speaking of, the second episode that comes to mind when reflecting on season five, is "A Hole in the World." My hatred for this episode is perfectly in harmony with home much I adore Winifred Burkle.

I hate this episode a LOT.

What you have to understand before watching a single episode of Buffy or Angel is that Joss Whedon hates love. Well, okay, to be precise Joss Whedon hates happiness. He loves using love as a means to an end but he hates seeing characters becoming happy and content because that's the antithesis of drama. I get it. I do. But after eight years of it...sigh. Sometimes you just want people to be happy, right?

I just can't help but notice that all the episodes that seem to love ripping my heart out are the ones that are directed by Joss, who does such a stellar job that you can't ever hate the episode despite how much you hate what is happening in front of you.

There are so many great moments in "A Hole in the World," like the "astronaut vs caveman" gag, the horrific "you are my sunshine" moment, Wes suddenly shooting a man's knee for not working the Fred case, the titular "hole" in the world, and the dual meaning behind it.

This episode is Angel's version of "The Body," but since Angel has always had a different dynamic and since the deceased in question is not just a B-character but an active member of the team (and arguably the purest of heart character in the whole universe), it hurts differently.

Also, since Angel is a different show that tells its stories different from Buffy, the layout of the episode is drastically altered: "The Body" starts with the death and then spends the episode processing it. This hits you with the inevitable news and then slowly marches you toward it. It brings out different shades of the same emotions. It's one of Joss' best episodes ever. It's magnificent. I cry like a baby every time I see it. It's great. It's a brilliant episode.

I hate it.

And then there's "Not Fade Away." This is it. This is the last episode, not only of Angel but of the whole Buffyverse. In that sense, you would think it would have a lot to carry on its shoulders, but it doesn't. Joss doesn't bother trying to wrap up two shows' worth of mythology. For one thing, he's already said adieu to Buffy (twice!). For another thing, he made this episode with the hope that there would be a sixth season.

In that sense, there was a lot less pressure here than there was with Buffy's "The Gift" or "Chosen." And yet, despite the possibility of more to come, the finale works as a fitting goodbye to the whole story of the "Vampire with a soul."

"Not Fade Away" is, first and foremost, a great finale, cliffhanger or not. In fact, despite the final shot, it's not really a cliffhanger at all. The only comparison it has to a cliffhanger is that it cuts away before the final fight occurs, meaning we lose the resolution to the action that's about to unfold.

Instead, everyone got their closure and resolution before the fight. Especially poignant was Wes' death, ending a six-season run as the Buffyverse's most well-developed and brilliantly evolved character. His final moments with Illyria's "Fred" put me in tears in a way an Angel episode hadn't since, you guessed it, "A Hole in the World." It's no surprise that both moments feature Fred. Spike's poetry reading was excellent too. Everyone had a chance to shine here and though I hate the way Lorne's run ended. I understood it.

All that said, as fitting an end to the series this episode is, it ends with me wanting more, something I didn't have after the sense of finality that Buffy's season 5 and season 7 finales offered. Buffy was ready to go after 5 seasons. It came back with a solid two-year coda and then, again, was ready to go after 7 seasons. I felt okay saying goodbye to her show, but not this time: Angel was not ready to go. There was a lot left in the tank for these guys and gals but as it was, it was a great ending to a great season of a great show.

And while it is easy to attack the episode for ending the way it did, especially in hindsight with the show not being renewed for a sixth season, I think it works perfectly in light of the theme of the series itself. Angel has always been about the fight, about the struggle, about what "knowing you have to get up and fight again" means to the fighter in question. It's not about the battle (that's for Buffy), it's about what the inevitability and endlessness of the battle does to you.

After five years—and especially after a year working for Wolfram & Hart—it's important that Angel, faced with overwhelming odds and a depleted army beside him, picks up his weapon and just says "I'm gonna go slay a dragon..." as the show fades to black.

Does he slay the dragon? Does he die? Forget the comic book sequels, just in terms of the show and the message it conveyed over the course of those five years, the point of the ending is that it doesn't matter whether Angel won or lost, lived or died. What matters is that he fought. He's a vampire, a demon of darkness and a minion of evil, and as long as he lived again, he chose to fight for good.

Along the way, we got to watch him fight that fight, struggle against the darkness, make some terrible mistakes, enjoy some triumphant victories, suffer some difficult losses and, ultimately, pick himself up to fight again, and again, and again. If you somehow don't think there's a lesson in that, an inspiring application to take from that, then at least Joss Whedon and co. gave us 110 episodes of fun, of action, of drama, of heartbreak, and of delightful characters and character growth, arguably better than you'll find on any show anywhere.

Thanks for the memories, Angel Investigations.

Chapter Thirteen

EVERY BUFFY RANKED 8/10

What else is left to say about the series I love so much? All that's left is to offer a completely biased, wholly unscientific, and absolutely indisputable ranking. So, without further ado here is part one of five in a list breaking down all 131 episodes of Buffy the Vampire Slayer.

Technically there were 144 episodes of the show produced but I'm combining a few two-parters because, though they aired on different weeks and sometimes had different writers/directors, they tell a single story spread across the two episodes. Things also get hairy when you get to the second half of season seven, where the stories get very serialized, but for the most part, even those episodes are still treated as single entries.

The list is divided into four categories (with a fifth chapter wholly devoted to the number one entry): At the bottom are the episodes "EIGHT AND BELOW." Those are the ones—ranked an 8/10 or below—that, for one reason or another, had serious missteps, structural flaws, bad plots, or some other errors that couldn't be overlooked no matter how charming the writing was.

After that, there are the episodes that are "NOT BAD BUT NOT MUCH." These episodes—ranked 8.5/10—all have plenty of redeeming qualities but they're hamstrung by one or two big problems or even a ton of little problems that keep it from rising up the ranks.

Next are the 9/10 episodes simply called "GEMS." These are the brilliant ones, the side-splittingly hilarious ones, the fantastically written ones, the surprise-filled twisty ones. These are the ones I loved, but not as much as the last group in the ranking.

At the top are "TENS." These are the 10/10 ones, the best of the best, the little pocket masterpieces that made the show the cult hit it became, and which helped the show maintain its place in genre fandom twenty-five years later.

Disclaimer #1: I won't be doing too much summarizing of the episodes here. Instead, I'll mostly spend the few words I have devoted to each entry explaining its placement in the ranking. This listing is for the fans, not someone who hasn't yet seen the show. What are you waiting for? Go watch the show!

Disclaimer #2: Making this list was, at times, a ton of fun and, at other times, agonizing. The best of the best were quickly identified, though coming up with a satisfactory ranking wasn't easy. Likewise, the bottom of the barrel episodes were also easily spotted, but which goes at the bottom?

Actually, that was easy, too...

BUFFY THE VAMPIRE SLAYER

THE "EIGHT AND BELOW" EPISODES

#131 – WRECKED
SEASON 6, EPISODE 10

The worst for multiple reasons. To start with, there is almost nothing to enjoy here. For another thing, the "magic is like drugs" parable is laid on so heavy-handedly, without nuance or subtext, it becomes secondhand embarrassing to watch. The scene where Willow drives "drunk" with Dawn in the passenger seat never sat right with me from a "true to character" standpoint.

#130 – BEER BAD
SEASON 4, EPISODE 5

A public service episode with a moronic plot. Don't get me wrong, there are plenty of episodes of Buffy and Angel that have silly plots, but the shows usually knew how to balance the silliness of it with a wink and a nod and some sharp writing to make you laugh with it and not at it. I didn't even laugh at beer bad. As with Wrecked, I was more embarrassed to watch.

MATTHEW L. MARTIN

#129 – SMASHED
SEASON 6, EPISODE 9

I almost combined this one with Wrecked, but I hated the latter one so much more and found this one less offensive enough to keep them split. For one, the hijinks of the trio is handled better than in other episodes. For another, the destructive relationship between Buffy and Spike is literalized in the most literal way possible. It's an episode with very little meaningful plot but a lot of good character development for everyone but Willow. She has development, just not the good kind.

#128 – I ROBOT YOU JANE
SEASON 1, EPISODE 8

We did not know how the internet worked in 1995. The plot is simple: Willow falls in love with a "person" on the internet, but the person is actually a demon that was, long ago, sealed in a book via magic (fine so far). That book was then uploaded onto a computer (uh...). And that set the demon loose in the computer (oh no...). And then the demon started online chatting with Willow (and now you lost me).

BUFFY THE VAMPIRE SLAYER

What follows is a lot of cringe, though I'm sure it wasn't so bad in 1995. I honestly can't remember. I do remember cringing pretty hard last year when I rewatched it.

#127 – SOME ASSEMBLY REQUIRED
SEASON 2, EPISODE 2

Students are being killed and reassembled as a Frankenstein's Monster-like creature. That's a pass. There's some nice Angel/Buffy stuff here, and some lovely Giles/Ms. Calendar flirting. In fact, that's a recurring theme to the first half of season 2: The plots are usually forgettable but the character stuff keeps things flowing nicely. The A-plot is enough of a bore to hold this one back, however.

#126 – THE PACK
SEASON 1, EPISODE 6

The problem with all the subpar season one episodes is the writers and actors hadn't quite figured out the needed subtleties to make everything work. These were very plot-centered episodes early on and the plots were not great. The Pack is about school bullying, with Xander and some other high schoolers being possessed by the spirit of wolves or something. It's just as on the nose as the next entry on the list, but not nearly as cheesy-fun.

#125 – TEACHER'S PET
SEASON 1, EPISODE 4

When you pitch a show to network execs, you usually have to offer up a handful of episode ideas to show how you can explore the various themes you intend to build the series around. Buffy was pitched as "High School is Hell... literally."

The personal demons and challenges young people face in school are, in this show, made literal. So, it's not enough for Xander to be preyed upon by a horny teacher, the teacher has to be a literal praying mantis monster determined to eat him. I wonder if my feelings would be better if the monster wasn't a B-Movie rubber suit. I was never embarrassed, however; the cheesiness and cheapness of it were almost endearing.

BUFFY THE VAMPIRE SLAYER

#124 – NIGHTMARES
SEASON 1, EPISODE 10

This one is a lot higher on other lists I scanned over the past year. Personally, I thought it was just an okay episode. I can see the hints at the kind of show Buffy would be, one that was willing to blur genre lines. The gimmick of turning the Scoobies' nightmares against them is a good idea, but it will be done much better in a later episode. This is just okay.

#123 – GO FISH
SEASON 2, EPISODE 20

The worst episodes of season 2 feel like they belonged to season 1. My problem with this episode is two-fold. On the one hand, the plot is season 1 levels of dumb, coming after the show had already jumped to a new level of quality, proving it was better than the kind of on-the-nose storytelling seen previously. The other problem is that the episode aired right before the amazing two-part finale.

This episode is sandwiched between two incredible stories (I Only Have Eyes For You, and Becoming 1-2) and sticks out like a sore thumb, ruining the flow that the show was on since Angel turned into Angelus. Rape jokes are also way too casually employed, but that's the mid-90s for you.

#122 – KILLED BY DEATH
SEASON 2, EPISODE 18

Feels like an idea that was bandied about when the writers were trying to nail down the plot of Nightmares. As with the previous entry, its biggest sin is that it stops the momentum of the Angelus storyline for a one-off that's not good enough to justify its placement in the season.

The episode also suffers from a bad writing trope: Introducing backstory that is only relevant in this episode and never brought up again. Buffy had a cousin who died in a hospital and now Buffy hates hospitals. She will be in hospitals a lot in this show so it's a good thing she completely conquers her fear here and now and never brings it up again.

#121 – GET IT DONE
SEASON 7, EPISODE 15

Season 7 is hardly a perfect year. I defended it in the write-up while noting that it is not without flaws. Its biggest sin is in the middle stretch of episodes, where it feels like the writers had run out of story, and were stretching things to the point of insanity just to fill out the twenty-two-episode quota.

The good news is this is the last episode before things turn around and pick up the momentum on the way to the finale. It's a whole lot of nothing here, though. Buffy hops into a portal to learn the origin story of the Slayers. A demon hops out of that portal to give Spike something to fight. The end. On its own, it's not terrible, but coming after a handful of episodes where very little happened to advance the story dragged it down.

#120 – INCA MUMMY GIRL
SEASON 2, EPISODE 4

Another season 2 episode that belongs in season 1: Xander falls for...well the title says it all.

#119 – SHADOW – SEASON 5, EPISODE 8

This is the one where Buffy fights the snake monster that looks like a season 1 costume. When the highlight of the episode is a laughably bad fight with a rubber snake monster, there's not much else to say.

MATTHEW L. MARTIN

#118 – BAD EGGS
SEASON 2, EPISODE 12

This episode only works when you see the subtext as a set-up for what comes in the next episode. This one teaches the lesson that "sex has consequences." Watching it live you would never imagine such a plot point would have such a disastrous and season-shaking payoff in the very next episode. Here it's just a silly story that sends up Alien and Invasion of the Body Snatchers to subpar results.

#117 – NEVER KILL A BOY
        ON THE FIRST DATE
SEASON 1, EPISODE 5

I think my biggest problem with season 1 is that it hadn't yet figured out the flow of a typical Buffy episode. The A and B plots tend to work against each other instead of complimenting each other as they will in, say, season 3.

Here, however, the problem is not a conflict between the two plots but it's the lack of a B plot entirely. There are two things going on here: Buffy trying to date Owen and Buffy needing to stop the rise of a prophesied big bad vamp. There is no jumping from one plot to the other, however. Both feature Buffy so the story ends up being told in a very monotonous way.

#116 – WHERE THE WILD THINGS ARE
SEASON 4, EPISODE 18

This is the episode that features Buffy and Riley getting it on in a Frat House that seems to feed off the getting-on of Buffy and Riley. I'm pretty firmly in the "hate Riley" camp so my annoyance with the episode cannot be overstated. I liked it from a visual standpoint; director David Solomon did some trippy things here. The story is bunk, however.

#115 – REPTILE BOY
SEASON 2, EPISODE 5

Buffy and Cordy go to a college frat party, are date raped, and are nearly eaten by a monster the frat boys worship. That's it. That's the episode. Great Cordy and Buffy banter keep it from falling any lower.

MATTHEW L. MARTIN

#114 – GONE
SEASON 6, EPISODE 11

Buffy cuts her hair. Buffy turns invisible. Buffy acts wildly out of character vs the rest of the season. Gone is just a tonally confused mess of an episode.

#113 – DOUBLEMEAT PALACE
SEASON 6, EPISODE 12

I so wanted to put this one higher on the list. It's very much a guilty pleasure episode in how bananas it gets in the end. It takes too long to get there, however, and if you're one of those people predisposed to hate season 6, you'll probably give up on the episode long before it gets hilariously cheesy for the big climactic fight.

The first half of the episode has too much of the moping around and depression that makes season 6 so polarizing. I don't think it's a particularly good episode, but I do have a soft spot for it.

BUFFY THE VAMPIRE SLAYER

#112 – REAL ME
SEASON 5, EPISODE 2

As with Doublemeat Palace, this one has a place in my heart, if only because Harmony makes for such a fun villainous foil. Buffy takes slaying so seriously (apart from the many quips) that a vapid moron like Harmony is precisely the kind of baddie that would get under her skin.

Other than the gags, however, there's really nothing to the episode. We don't yet know what is going on with Dawn, who she is, why she is, etc, and it's not yet intriguing enough to carry that half of the story.

#111 – GINGERBREAD
SEASON 3, EPISODE 11

It's a testament to how strong and consistent season 3 is that it only has two entries in the bottom quarter of the rankings. Gingerbread has one amazing moment, with Buffy impaling a demon via a large wooden stake attached to her back. She has to bend over to pierce the baddie through the neck, meaning at first she doesn't know if she did the deed or not. The way Sarah Michelle Geller says "did I get it?" is perfect, followed by Xander and Oz busting through the ceiling in their attempt to save the day. As with everything else in season three, the tone is perfect, but the plot here is a bit too silly to work.

#110 – LISTENING TO FEAR
SEASON 5, EPISODE 9

Fair or not, my biggest problem with the episode is that the monster in question is not a monster or a traditional demon or some other hellspawn but is, in fact, an alien from outer space. It is, unless I'm forgetting something, the only such time a villain in the show has been interstellar. I know it's called a demon in the show, and is even described as being "summoned" but it came from the stars! What a weird way to do that. There are some good moments here, which is expected since season 5 is abundant with great little character moments. It's the stitching that binds it all that's lacking.

#109 – FIRST DATE
SEASON 7, EPISODE 14

As said already, this episode falls in that middle stretch of episodes in season 7 where things grind to a halt. There are plot developments stretched out over the whole episode here that, in earlier years, would have been handled in a scene or two.

Buffy and Principal Wood go out on a date and Buffy realizes Wood has some skills fighting vamps. Meanwhile, Xander goes out on a date with early-2000s singing sensation Ashanti. She ends up trying to sacrifice him in a pagan ritual because of course she does; Xander's luck with women is hilariously terrible. There's too much padding and filler in these episodes. Watching them in a row actually helps; seeing them piecemeal is a slog.

#108 – ALL THE WAY
SEASON 6, EPISODE 6

Buffy's Halloween episodes in seasons 2 and 4 were standouts. Season 6 focuses on Dawn and features a plot that feels like a throwback to the simpler days of season 1 and the first half of season 2 (going out on a date and wanting that first kiss from someone who turns out to be a vampire). Considering how far the show had grown to this point, I don't know if a throwback feel is what was needed here.

There are things to praise, particularly in how it continues to plant seeds that will be watered as the season progresses and the worst traits of the Scoobies become their undoing. That's a staple of every other episode in the first half of season 6 however, and it's handled better in those outings than here.

#107 – BEAUTY AND THE BEASTS
SEASON 3, EPISODE 4

The story here is a good one: People are being killed, it's around the full moon, so naturally, Oz is a suspect. The audience, however, is led to suspect it is the recently-returned Angel, who is acting far less human than he was in season 2. The Angel story ends up being a clever red herring, though the actual villain is a bit underwhelming. Oz was always a great character, but the episodes which put him in the center of the action usually underwhelmed. He worked better as the laid-back guy making wise and funny observations.

#106 – TED
SEASON 2, EPISODE 11

Ted is another polarizing episode in the Buffy fandom. For me, I like a lot all the pieces but not the whole of it. John Ritter is great. The

BUFFY THE VAMPIRE SLAYER

basic idea is good too. The mid-episode turn is really well-done, but the ultimate payoff as to who (what) Ted is, comes off to me as too out of left field. As with the rest of season 2's weaker entries, it feels like an idea rejected in season 1, though the production and overall quality is a step up from the year before. Ultimately, it's a lot of good set-up with an ending that falls flat.

#105 – CHECKPOINT
SEASON 5, EPISODE 12

This episode serves two purposes: It gives us some nice conflict between Buffy and the Watchers, a dynamic missing since the days of Faith and Wesley in season 3. It also builds to the final line(s) of the episode, where Buffy is finally told what it is she's dealing with in Glory: "She's not a demon...she's a god." To that Buffy responds, in her perfectly Buffy way: "Oh."

The highlight of the episode is the "power" speech Buffy gives, which gets a big cheer from the rest of the Scoobies. It's a great scene, but it's the only really great scene in the episode. The rest is unremarkable.

MATTHEW L. MARTIN

#104 – LESSONS
SEASON 7, EPISODE 1

Buffy's first episodes of each season are never high-water marks for the year: Usually they're too busy establishing themes that will be explored for the remainder of the season. Season 7 will end with a whopper of a finale, but it begins almost like the pilot of a spinoff show.

Buffy returns to Sunnydale High and takes up a teaching position, we meet some new kids that look like potential series leads, and a threat is introduced (cryptically) to establish the stakes. If you told me Netflix was reviving the show, that's the kind of episode I can see kicking it off. It landed weird and while it's not bad, it's too focused on planting seeds to be a compelling episode on its own.

#103 – WILD AT HEART
SEASON 4, EPISODE 6

Oz had his character assassinated by Joss Whedon as punishment for his desire to leave the show. That's the only explanation I can give to the idea that Oz would ever cheat on Willow, especially when there were a dozen other ways to go about writing him off the show. They did Oz dirty and while a lot of the episode is good and well-done, the ending—and the way they got there—brings down the whole of it.

Chapter Fourteen

EVERY BUFFY RANKED 8.5/10

These are the episodes that are better all-around than the ones previously discussed, while still lacking that little something extra to put them in the higher tier. There are some fun ones to consider here, however, including more than a few that almost made ranked high enough to be featured in the next chapter's set of episodes. Still, what we have here is a set of episodes without any true misfires...

BUFFY THE VAMPIRE SLAYER

#102 – THE DARK AGE
SEASON 2, EPISODE 8

The best part about this episode is the reveal that Giles wasn't always a stuck-up goody-two-shoes. He was once a very dark magic dabbler and now his past has come back to haunt him. It's a fairly commonly-used story to tell, but there's enough heart and charm here to keep things interesting. It helps that Anthony Stewart Head (who played Giles) is so easily likable and charming it makes the rare times when he becomes the focus of the episode that much more interesting.

#101 – BARGAINING 1-2
SEASON 6, EPISODES 1-2

The first episodes of the UPN era kicked off with a literal resurrection of the heroine. There's a good balance of humor and horror here, and some genuine shocks (Willow slaughtering the innocent deer brought a gasp out of me the first time I saw it).

The build-up to Buffy's actual resurrection is deftly handled as well, saving it for the final moment of the first half. There's so much here that is only appreciated with the benefit of hindsight; when you consider the overall storyline and themes of season six, a lot of the writing choices in the opening make sense. At the time it was seen simply as a good, but not great, re-debut for the Slayer.

#100 – CRUSH
SEASON 5, EPISODE 14

Spike's love for Buffy is one of those things where you simply can't see it coming until it happens, and when it happens suddenly every clue you never noticed smacks you in the face. Of course he would fall for Buffy, not just because of who she is but who he is.

Spike is exactly the kind of vampire that would fall for her, and their relationship (which certainly does not begin here, if ever, but is at least "changed" here) is infinitely more interesting (and messy) than the "forbidden love" thing she has with Angel. Spike and Buffy are "twin flames" and the first inkling of that previously-improbable truth is shown here...in an episode where Spike kidnaps Buffy and tries to force her to admit she has feelings for him too. As I said, it's messy but rarely boring.

BUFFY THE VAMPIRE SLAYER

#99 – THE WITCH
SEASON 1, EPISODE 3

TV shows don't really "start" until the episode that airs after the premiere. There's always a special quality to the "first" episode as everything is new and introduced. What comes next is when the audience gets a sense of whether or not the show will succeed.

Buffy's third episode features the heroine tangling with a witch on the cheerleading team, only to discover that the villain is actually the cheerleader's mother, possessing the body of her daughter. It's an added layer to the plot that didn't have to happen; a lesser show could have just kept things confined to a simple "freak of the week" to be defeated, but Buffy's writers went the extra mile, gave us a memorable ending, and proved the show would be more than just fluff.

#98 – TOUCHED
SEASON 7, EPISODE 20

There's not a lot going on, plot-wise here, but what this episode has is the most beautiful monologue in the series, as Spike explains to Buffy what it is that makes her so special. There's not much else to say about the episode, but that speech alone is enough to make it memorable.

#97 – WHEN SHE WAS BAD
SEASON 2, EPISODE 1

Season two is a tale of two halves, with the second half kicking off a tremendous leap in quality so notable the show is almost unrecognizable before and after. That said, the first half of season two offers a few hints here and there that promise an uptick in quality compared to season one. Most episodic adventure shows wouldn't have dwelled too heavily on the happenings of the previous episode, but Buffy kicked off its second season with the heroine undergoing severe post-traumatic stress. She technically died and was brought back to life; that sticks with you, and Buffy has a hard time coping with it. What follows is an episode that is better in its ideas than its execution, but its ideas are great and its execution is not bad.

#96 – NORMAL AGAIN
SEASON 6, EPISODE 17

An episode like this—with Buffy seemingly losing her mind and wondering if she is really a normal girl in an insane asylum who has delusions of being the slayer—can easily be done in a hackneyed and eye-rolling way.

In fact, if there's a line between being hackneyed on the one side and something as sublime and brilliant as DS9's "Far Beyond the Stars" on the other, this one falls more on the hackneyed side. It does the job okay, but it never rises above the cliched concept.

#95 – NEW MOON RISING
SEASON 4, EPISODE 19

Oz didn't exactly get a nice ending as a series regular in season three, but he gets a comeback here and a chance to leave the show with a bit more dignity. I say that, despite the fact that the plot centers around him having violent mood swings as he struggles to keep his werewolf persona in check. It's at least a plotline that doesn't betray who he is as a character. He was trying to do the right thing but it went bad; that's much better than needlessly sleeping with a rando werewolf lady while being involved with Willow. The B-plot is the Adam/Initiative nonsense that is better left unspoken.

MATTHEW L. MARTIN

#94 – CHOICES
SEASON 3, EPISODE 19

The highlight here is the showdown between the Mayor and the Scoobies at Sunnydale. Coming so close to the finale, but not yet the finale, made this have an "anything can happen" sort of feel. Most of the episode is just concerned with moving plot pieces around and setting things up for the big season-ending finale, but that one scene at the school was enough to put this one higher up on the list than it otherwise would have been.

#93 – NEVER LEAVE ME
SEASON 7, EPISODE 9

The episode pulls off two things: First, it reveals for us the big bad for the season, and second, it illustrates the unwillingness of Buffy to write off Spike, despite how violent he has become (under the influence of the First). Buffy can't deny her feelings for him and refuses to dust him, insisting that he needs help. That one admission creates a throughline that will carry the viewer to the finale of the show, making this one an important episode, even if it's a bit skimpy on actual plot (a running problem with much of season seven).

#92 – THE KILLER IN ME
SEASON 7, EPISODE 13

So, when I say season seven struggled with plots, what I mean is the individual story that lasts the duration of the episode. A lot of season seven episodes had very little in the way of plots. Instead, they were just interconnected scenes that dealt with the big bad arc of the whole year. This one is an exception, and it's not a great one. It focuses on Willow's appearance changing into Warren's, the result of a spell cast by the returning Amy. While the character really soured on me in season six, I am at least appreciative that she received closure here in the final season. The plot isn't much, but it's at least something, which is more than can be said for about half of the season's episodes.

#91 – THE FRESHMAN
SEASON 4, EPISODE 1

Buffy's greatest strength as a show is how delicately it balances the physical strength of the heroine with the vulnerabilities of her still being a teenage girl. She can punch a hole in a concrete wall without breaking a sweat, but she can also turn into a puddle over a bad relationship. She's superhuman...and also human. Her vulnerable side is on display in the opening of season four, which sees Buffy starting college and being taken advantage of by a sleazy older student. If he were a demon she could pummel him into dust, but he's just a jerk, so all she can do is be sad. She's helpless and we are helpless to watch it. It's not the best first episode in the show, but it's a strong outing and one that does a good job resetting things after the old high school setting was blown up in the previous episode.

#90 – FAITH HOPE TRICK
SEASON 3, EPISODE 3

Season three takes a few episodes to goof around before it really settles into its arc, but in those opening episodes, we meet some delightful new characters. One of them is the vampire Trick, and the other—more importantly—is Faith, the Vampire Slayer. Faith will become arguably the most important side-character in the series, and one of the most beloved. She's introduced to us here with all the attitude, cockiness, and confidence that will come to define the character (at least on the surface) for years to come. Her chemistry with Buffy is instantaneous.

#89 – NO PLACE LIKE HOME
SEASON 5, EPISODE 5

First, there's the plot, which gives us our first hint at the big bad for the season and sheds a little more light on the nature of Dawn (with still many unanswered questions left hanging). That's all fine and good. Perfectly cromulent. What really sells the episode for me, however, is the magical exchange between Spike and Buffy when she asks what he's doing skulking around her house, and wants his answer in five words or less. Spike's answer: "Out for a walk...b*tch."

Twin flames.

#88 – DOOMED
SEASON 4, EPISODE 11

This one is knee-deep in the Initiative arc, but while that usually is an instant turn-off for me, what works here is the fast pace and the many twists in the story as it progresses. This is the episode that immediately follows Hush, where

Buffy and Riley discover the other is more than they suspected. Here we get the fallout, which happens amidst the backdrop of a demon invasion. Concentrate on the action, tune out the pseudo-military crap that makes the Initiative stuff such a drag, and this is a perfectly fine episode.

#87 – EMPTY PLACES
SEASON 7, EPISODE 19

Two things of note happen here. First, Buffy is kicked out of her own house, which infuriates me every time I watch it. It's such a short-sighted move and feels like a character-betrayal to everyone present. I hate it hate it hate it. If Spike had been there he never would have allowed it to happen.

And where was Spike? He was on a motorcycle with Andrew, on their way to hunt for clues about the First's henchman, Caleb that leads to the second thing of note in this episode, the bonding that happens between these two unlikely friends over a bloomin' onion...

BUFFY THE VAMPIRE SLAYER

#86 – WELCOME TO HELLMOUTH
& THE HARVEST
SEASON 1, EPISODES 1-2

First episodes do not always accurately reflect the quality of a TV series. Buffy didn't become "Buffy" until mid-way through season two, and the show didn't really hit its high-water mark until season three, but all the things that make the show great are still here on display in the very first episodes.

The opening, with Darla playing the part of a seeming damsel in distress, about to be attacked by a blood-sucking fiend, only to flip the script and reveal herself to be the danger, is still a fabulously-done subversion of the cliched trope. Considering how the whole series is built around subverting the idea of the damsel in distress, and showing her to be the ultimate hero, starting the show with a damsel that is really a villain was a stroke of brilliance.

The rest of the two-part opening is a standard 90s adventure TV set-up. It reminds me a lot of the Smallville opening episodes in how it methodically establishes the characters, the destiny of the hero, and a small threat to overcome to whet the appetite and get the viewer to come back. The show will improve by leaps and bounds in episodes to come, but it nevertheless had a pretty solid start.

#85 – OUT OF SIGHT OUT OF MIND
SEASON 1, EPISODE 11

Season one episodes all have a different kind of charm compared to the rest of the series. It's probably because all the episodes were written and filmed before anything had aired, so there was no audience feedback to take into consideration.

The show was just what they set it out to be and nothing more. The penultimate episode of the season is very cliched and very much in keeping with the "high school is hell" theme. Who among us hasn't felt invisible in high school? At Sunnydale, that's a feeling that is made literal. The result is an episode about as good as the average season one outing. It's fine, but not much else.

#84 – ENTROPY
SEASON 6, EPISODE 18

You know how Buffy repeatedly told Spike she was not interested in a real relationship? And remember how Xander literally left Anya at the altar? Well, in this episode, both are furious to see Anya and Spike making out. That's it. That's the episode. It's good.

#83 – THE PUPPET SHOW
SEASON 1, EPISODE 9

There are a few episodes of BTVS that polarize the fanbase, episodes that some hate and some adore. I know more than a few who completely dismiss this episode but, for all the criticism season one rightly deserves, I can't help but love this weird tale of a possessed ventriloquist dummy.

There's something about the way the episode ends with a casual conversation between Buffy and the dummy, the matter-of-fact way the villain speaks, despite his mouth just going up and down like a...well, like a dummy. It's all so bizarre. It's something that would only have been done in season one and I can't help but dig it.

#82 – INTO THE WOODS
SEASON 5, EPISODE 10

Goodbye Riley. The episode leading up to the climactic moment when the derpy goober finally flew off into the proverbial sunset was nothing spectacular. In fact, it was flat-out regressive at times, with Buffy running to him desperate to patch things up when it was really Riley that was in the wrong. Whatever. The sight of him flying away, out of the show for good (but for a one-off a year later) was all I needed to rank this one as high as it is.

#81 – ANNE
SEASON 3, EPISODE 1

Season one ended with Buffy dying (for a sec). Season two opened with Buffy dealing with the PTSD that followed. Season two ended with Buffy running a sword through the heart of her lover. If you didn't think season three would deal with the emotional fallout of that, you haven't been paying attention.

Buffy ran away from home and ended up in a hell dimension. The plot itself is pretty forgettable but the episode's willingness to show the title character's aforementioned vulnerable side remains its great strength and makes for a solid start to the best overall season of the series.

#80 – HELPLESS
SEASON 3, EPISODE 12

At the heart of this episode is the quasi-father/daughter relationship between Giles and Buffy. Going in, after two or so years together, the two had grown very close, to the point where viewers could be forgiven for thinking of Giles as a surrogate father to Buffy. Then we find out he is willing to drug her and strip her of her powers to test her as per the Watcher's Code.

The gross violation of Buffy's person rightly hurts not only her but the viewer (and Giles, once his guilt takes over). It's almost as if the writers wanted to pull back on the "surrogate father" idea, especially since the episode's sub-plot features Buffy waiting for her real father to return for an annual ice-skating trip. When he doesn't show, we all sit in front of our TVs waiting for Giles to take her...but he never does.

Giles ends up being fired as a Watcher because they say he's too close to Buffy. And yet, when it's time for someone to take Buffy to the Ice Show, Giles doesn't step up: He isn't her father, and this episode—painful but well-made—hammers that fact home for us.

#79 – HOMECOMING
SEASON 3, EPISODE 5

Slayerfest '98 is a fun idea and a good use of Trick, but it's the relationship between Buffy and Cordy that carries the episode. Those two were natural enemies in the show's early going but season three is the year where they start to become close and Cordy actually becomes a Scooby.

The turning point of that change is this episode, which sees the two girls feuding over which one can become Homecoming Queen. It's a rare thing to see Buffy be so vapid, but it won't be the last time her obsessive tendencies come out. The result here is an action-heavy episode with surprisingly strong character development (and a fun ending).

#78 – BRING ON THE NIGHT
& SHOWTIME
SEASON 7, EPISODES 10-11

The scene of Buffy searching for "evil" on the internet, in search of tips on how to defeat "The First" is one of my favorite gags on a series replete with little one-off gags. It also works on a separate level, however, as it illustrates the near-futility in trying to fight something that has no corporeal form and cannot, technically, be killed. How do you even begin to fight the whole concept of evil itself? Buffy starts with a word search. I get it.

The first half of this two-parter ends with Buffy getting beat up pretty badly by an ubervamp, and just when we think she's about to launch into another one of her dreaded season seven speeches, she tells the heroes to suit up and come with her for a fight. That takes us to part two, which is perhaps the episode most devoid of plot in the whole series.

Buffy fights the ubervamp in a sort of makeshift gladiator ring and, after a struggle, takes off its head. They might not be able to kill "evil" but they can take out evil's minions. That's a start. The two-parter offers little by way of plot, but it has some good humor in part one and good action in part two. The whole of it is better than the parts.

#77 – AS YOU WERE
SEASON 6, EPISODE 15

Midway through season six saw Buffy at a very low point, so what better way to kick a heroine when she's doing than by bringing back her ex-boyfriend who seems not only happily moved on with his life, but 100% improved since the breakup. This is easily the best use of Riley in the whole series, which isn't saying much, and it's probably because there's a good story being told with Buffy that Riley is integral to, something he often wasn't when he was a main-star.

MATTHEW L. MARTIN

#76 – DEAD MAN'S PARTY
SEASON 3, EPISODE 2

On the one hand, the episode is little more than fluff. It's a basic monster mash romp of an episode with no real weighty stakes or world-threatening danger on the line. It's about a zombie outbreak in Sunnydale for crying out loud. But, in classic Buffy style, the show takes the cliched and makes it too charming, too funny, and too much fun to roll your eyes at. This is the episode that spawned this amazing line from an exasperated Giles...

"'Oh do you like my mask? Isn't it pretty? It raises the dead.'......Americans."

I almost pushed it to a higher ranking just for that.

#75 – OUT OF MY MIND
SEASON 5, EPISODE 4

A lot is going on here and while the different pieces don't really mesh together into a tight cohesive unit, each of them are entertaining in their own right. There's the revelation that Riley is doping to get stronger to keep up with

Buffy, which further exposes what a terrible person he is. Good stuff there.

There's the beginning of the Joyce/brain tumor subplot that will last for much of season five and will lead to some great dramatic moments, and one of the absolute best episodes of the series. And there's the dream Spike has about making out with Buffy, which wakes him up in a start, shocked and mortified at what his subconscious has revealed to him. Good parts, not necessarily a great whole.

#74 – VILLAINS
SEASON 6, EPISODE 20

This is a heavy episode. Tara is dead. Buffy is injured by a bullet. Willow has gone nuts with anger. A lot is going on and there are some great moments here, including the scene where Willow removes the bullet from Buffy using magic. Spike is gone, off to hunt for a soul, Buffy leaves Dawn in the care of Clem, Xander is no help (as per usual); everything feels like it's spiraling out of control.

The climax of the episode features Willow literally flaying Warren alive (though the deed almost instantly kills him) as punishment for murdering Tara. It's dark. In a season whose whole theme is sending the Scoobies to rock bottom, this is it. We've hit rock bottom. Now we have to spend a few episodes just wallowing around in it.

#73 – THE 1 IN TEAM
& GOODBYE IOWA
SEASON 4, EPISODES 13-14

Buffy struggles juggling her time with Riley and the Initiative with her time as a Slayer and with the Scoobies. Considering how little Riley offers as a character compared to the Scooby Gang, and considering how cringy and embarrassing the Initiative is compared to how funny and charming the Scooby Gang is, it's reeeeeally hard for me to see the struggle here.

Things come to a head when the leader of the Initiative tries to kill Buffy, forcing Riley in the follow-up episode to choose between the goobers and the Scoobies. I wish he had chosen poorly, but he chose team-Scoob. Whatever. This was the two-parter that introduces us to Adam, the replacement baddie because the Initiative arc had been going so badly (and the central villain requested to leave the show) that they had to call an audible.

BUFFY THE VAMPIRE SLAYER

#72 – THE INITIATIVE
SEASON 4, EPISODE 7

Spike made his big comeback one episode earlier, but that was at the very end of the episode; now we get his big return in all its glory. It takes something "other" to make the Initiative-heavy episodes any good, and having Spike return after a year away is like a breath of fresh air in a previously-stale environment. He's got a chip in his head that makes him incapable of attacking humans, which leads to a hilarious discovery while trying to attack Willow. To say the show missed Spike is an understatement.

MATTHEW L. MARTIN

Chapter Fifteen

EVERY BUFFY RANKED 9/10

Already we have considered the episodes ranked 8/10 or below. Those are the bottom-of-the-barrel episodes, though there are only a few would I consider bad, and basically, none of these have anything positive to offer during a rewatch.

After that we looked at the episodes ranked 8.5/10, the ones that aren't bad but they lack the little extra something that makes Buffy's best episodes so magical. From here on out, though, we're looking at the cream of the crop episodes, the ones ranked 9/10. Each one is a treat, either because it's so funny, so clever, so scary, or any combination thereof. They're not the absolute best of the best, 10/10 episodes, but they're almost that good. These are...

THE GEMS

#71 – WHAT'S MY LINE 1-2
SEASON 2, EPISODES 9-10

"What's My Line" is the only official two-part episode in the show (not counting a few premieres and finales). I'm not over the moon by it as it mostly felt like one and a half episodes with twenty minutes of material they couldn't cut to make it a single episode so they padded it out into two episodes. That said, there is a lot to love here.

The reveal of Kendra was a shock, the kiss between Xander and Cordy even more so, and the final shot of part 2, with an injured Spike being carried to safety by a fully-revived Drusilla is chilling every time I see it. Dru has always been the scarier threat between the two of them, and Juliet Landau never gets enough credit for all she brought to the role.

Buffy The Vampire Slayer S02e10 Juliet Landau James Marsters Drusilla Spike

MATTHEW L. MARTIN

#70 – PHASES
SEASON 2, EPISODE 15

First, Giles is getting absolutely giddy at the idea they will be tangling with a werewolf in this episode. *"It's one of the classics!"* he says with delight. Second, there's Oz's phone call to his Aunt Maureen, which perfectly captures the laid-back demeanor fans loved so much about him.

Earlier in the episode, we learn Oz was bit by his cousin Geordie. Being bit in a werewolf episode is a big red flag but since it was just his little cousin, we're led to believe it's just a red herring. But then Oz makes the call, just to check...

> *"Hey Aunt Maureen I wanted to ask you something? Is Geordie a werewolf?......uh huh.....and how long as that been going on?"*

Delightful. The episode's not much to write home about, but it's solid and fun from beginning to end.

BUFFY THE VAMPIRE SLAYER

#69 – DEAD THINGS
SEASON 6, EPISODE 13

Otherwise known as the one where the incel trio devises a mind control device to turn women into sex slaves. What starts as horny teenage fantasies (dressing a woman up as a maid to serve them drinks, etc) soon turns into something even darker, as the leader of the trio—Warren, easily the most despicable character in the series—makes a move toward rape.

A fight ensues and Warren kills her, then uses a rather convoluted series of events to trick Buffy into thinking she accidentally killed her while on patrol. Convoluted is the keyword here, but while the episode always threatens to go off the rails, it never totally does. It gets dark and uncomfortable, but that's just the name of the game this season.

#68 – TOUGH LOVE / SPIRAL
SEASON 5, EPISODES 19-20

I'm considering this a two-parter since, even though it doesn't have "to be continued" at the end of the first episode, it ends with as much of a cliffhanger as you could get, with Glory breaking into the Scooby's hangout and discovering Dawn is the key.

MATTHEW L. MARTIN

The follow-up features Giles driving an RV with the Scoobies in tow, trying to find a hiding place away from Glory, while also being pursued by what looks like cosplaying Templar Knights on horseback. The whole episode is surreal and fun, balancing out the dread that comes with knowing Glory is actively hunting them. The tension wouldn't have worked had the season not done such a great job conveying how much of a threat she is, setting the stage for the breathtaking finale.

#67 – DIRTY GIRLS
SEASON 7, EPISODE 18

Caleb joins the party as the necessary henchman of the Big Bad. Clever as it is to have a villain that can't be touched and thus can't be harmed, at some point the hero's gotta punch a fool.

Caleb is introduced to us as a twisted priest who wants to cleanse the sinners of the world in the most painful ways possible. He's a creepy, chilling, serial killer sort of villain, played to perfection by Nathan Fillion. The climax of the episode sees Caleb jab Xander's eye out of his head, making all those references to how much Xander "sees" in people in the weeks leading up to this moment all the more fitting.

BUFFY THE VAMPIRE SLAYER

#66 – OLDER AND FAR AWAY
SEASON 6, EPISODE 14

If the title doesn't jog your memory, this is the one where the whole gang is trapped in the Summers' house thanks to a spell by a vengeance demon. It's Buffy's 21st birthday and in keeping with the show's history, she doesn't get a happy celebration. Also, this being season six, everyone has a lot of personal drama to work through, so what better time and place than in a single location where no one has any privacy. The writers get a lot out of the limited setting, balancing the obvious humor and drama that would arise.

#65 – I WAS MADE TO LOVE YOU
SEASON 5, EPISODE 15

When you watch this episode for the first time it seems like a slight, mostly meaningless outing for the Slayer. If it accomplishes anything, it reinforces the infatuation Spike has developed toward Buffy. It's not until the final moments that the episode—which, that point, had been light-hearted and fun, sucker punches you in the gut and rips your heart out.

The final shot is one of the most shocking cliffhangers in television history, and it doesn't get the credit it deserves for that, simply because the episode leading up to it is so unrelated to the ending. We'll talk more about the next episode, "The Body" in the next chapter. This one is fun (until the ending).

#64– BLOOD TIES
SEASON 5, EPISODE 13

Blood Ties is one of those arc-heavy episodes that lacks much of a standout plot but does a good job building on the overall story of the season. If there's one thing happening here it's Dawn coming to realize she is the Key and not the normal human girl she always believed herself to be.

The highlight of the episode is a speech Buffy gives her, pointing out that Dawn bleeds the same blood she does, a factoid that seems like a nice thought and nothing more, but which will pay off in spades in the season finale.

BUFFY THE VAMPIRE SLAYER

#63 – BEWITCHED, BOTHERED, AND BEWILDERED
SEASON 2, EPISODE 16

Xander episodes either work or flop. Either way, they're almost certainly going to be dripping with late-90s teenage sexism. Xander gets dumped by Cordelia, attempts a love spell that makes everyone BUT Cordy fall for him, and then has to deal with the horny consequences. Needless to say, hijinks ensue. Your mileage may vary. I thought it was a ton of fun.

#62 – FLOODED
SEASON 6, EPISODE 4

Buffy turns a wrench on a pipe to fix a leak in their basement. The result is a flooded basement, giving the episode its title and giving us a metaphor for a life that feels like it's drowning in problems. Season six is a heavy one, but this one came early enough in the year for some fun to be had amidst all the angst. Buffy slicing her skirt to take out a baddie at the bank is a series-highlight-moment.

MATTHEW L. MARTIN

#61 – TRIANGLE
SEASON 5, EPISODE 11

Anya's ex-boyfriend Olaf the Troll makes his appearance in an episode that resolves the ongoing tension between Willow and Anya. Buffy's anger at Olaf's insinuation that Xander and Anya is a doomed relationship (due to her recent breakup with Riley) is fun, as is everything else about Olaf. Honestly, I'm sitting here wondering how this underrated gem isn't higher on my list? Olaf's comeback in season 7 is one of my favorite surprises of that year. He's great. More Olaf. Give me an Olaf spinoff series. I don't care if it's been a quarter-century.

#60 – LIE TO ME
SEASON 2, EPISODE 7

"Lie to Me" earns its title at the end of the episode. After having to stake a friend who turned into a vampire (willingly, as an escape from terminal cancer), she turns to Giles looking for comfort.

Knowing this world is evil and there is little comfort to share, she offers an alternative: "Lie to me." At which point he tells her the good guys are always loyal, the bad guys are always obvious, good always wins, no one ever has to die, and everyone lives happily ever after. It's quite a lie, especially in this show which seemed to revel in undermining those comforting ideas.

#59 – BUFFY VS DRACULA
SEASON 5, EPISODE 1

A showdown between our Vampire Slayer and the most famous vampire in history was either always going to happen or it was never going to happen. I can't decide if it was inevitable or if—had we never got this episode—it would have felt like a missed opportunity. I think I'm in the former camp.

I don't think Buffy needed a run-in with Dracula. In fact, before the episode aired, I had already decided that Dracula was long since dead, having been staked by Van Helsing or someone else ages ago. Instead, in this universe, Drac is unstakable and living off the fame of his name. I rate the episode as highly as I do because of what it is.

If I looked at it for what it wasn't, I probably would knock it down a few notches: This is the greatest vamp ever vs our hero, the Slayer. I expected more than a one-off episode that offers no real resolution. Dracula could have been a season-long big bad. Instead, he dips in and out in the season five premiere and is never heard from again. What we got is fun, though, I can't deny, especially Xander being under his spell.

#58 – THE WEIGHT OF THE WORLD
SEASON 5, EPISODE 21

This is one of those episodes that would never have been made had the show been produced in the era of 8-13 episode streaming shows. A twenty-two-episode season means you need "filler," but on Buffy, filler meant digging into the psyche of the character. In this case, that's all we do, as Willow goes inside Buffy's catatonic mind to help her come out of her funk and save the day. It's a thought-provoking, moving, and fascinating little episode, and I'm glad we have it.

#57 – BENEATH YOU
SEASON 7, EPISODE 2

Most of the plot is about a silly monster. The real treat here is the finale, which sees Spike finally confess to Buffy (in his own way) that he went searching for a soul so he might not ever again be the kind of person who would do what he tried to do in season 6's "Seeing Red." The things he says sound like bizarre ramblings but when you read the text you start to see the thought process...

Spike: I tried to find it, of course.

Buffy: *Find what?*

Spike: The spark. The missing... the piece... that fit. That would make me fit. Because you didn't want... God, I can't. Not with you looking. Angel—he should have warned me. He makes a good show of forgetting, but it's here, in me... all the time. The spark. I wanted to give you... what you deserve. And I got it. They put the spark in me. And now all it does is burn.

Buffy: *Your soul.*

Spike: Bit worse for lack of use.

Buffy: *You got your soul back. How?*

Spike: It's what you wanted, right? It's what you wanted, right?! And-and now everybody's in here, talking. Everything I did, everyone I— and him. And it. The other... the thing... beneath... beneath you. It's here, too. Everybody... they all just tell me go. Go... to hell.

Buffy: Why? Why would you do that?

Spike: Buffy, shame on you. Why does a man do what he mustn't? For her. To be hers. To be the kind of man who would nev—. To be a kind of man. And she shall look on him with forgiveness... and everybody will forgive and love. He will be loved. So everybody's okay, right? C-can we rest now? Buffy? Can we rest?

It's honestly one of the most beautiful scenes of the whole series. The rest of the episode is fine.

#56 – FAMILY
SEASON 5, EPISODE 6

What does it say that "Family" is the most run-of-the-mill, mundane, ho-hum episode Joss Whedon contributed to the show. It wasn't a big season opener or closer. It wasn't a hugely important, mid-season tone-shifter. It wasn't a special event that showed off the director's flair. It was just a really well-made episode, focusing on Tara and her psychologically abusive father.

Had anyone else's name appeared in the credits as director, the episode would probably be right where it is in the rankings. Lots of other people could have made this episode. You can't say that about "Hush" or "The Body." Forget all of that and just focus on the episode and it's really really good. That makes it low on the rankings for a Whedon episode, but halfway up the rankings overall.

#55 – HIM
SEASON 7, EPISODE 6

The first third of season seven is a delightful return to the classic era of Buffy episodes, with hijinks, comedy, goofy sci-fi/horror mash-ups, and more quips than you can keep up with. After the angst-heavy sixth season, the first seven or so episodes were a welcome breath of fresh air. Things get dark very soon after that, but the episode "Him" is the highlight of how fun the show could still be. The plot is almost season one levels of campy: a magic letterman jacket makes the girls go crazy. How the premise is applied is where the magic happens...

#54 – THE HARSH LIGHT OF DAY
SEASON 4, EPISODE 3

This is basically the last time we see classic old villain Spike and he goes out with quite the performance, finding a ring that essentially makes a vampire immune to all the things that could kill them (sunlight, stakes, etc). He's foiled, of course, because Spike's greatest character trait is being the most confident loser ever. The payoff is Oz gets to make a trip to Angel's bumpy first season and give that show a spark. It works too.

#53 – END OF DAYS
SEASON 7, EPISODE 21

The penultimate episode of the series is light on plot and heavy on set-up, but while that's usually a detriment, in this case, it works because the episode ends up being a series of "moments" that put all the pieces where they need to be for the finale. My favorite of these moments features Xander and Dawn in two scenes. In the first, he chloroforms her to drive her away from the dangerous battle to come. In the second, she puts a stun gun to his neck and drives back to the dangerous battle to come.

Dawn's come a long way.

#52 – BAD GIRLS & CONSEQUENCES
SEASON 3, EPISODES 14-15

In "Bad Girls" Faith plays the devil on Buffy's shoulder. At first, it's harmless, then it becomes a problem the others can see but which Buffy ignores, then Faith accidentally stabs a guy. Not a vamp; a man. When she expresses zero remorse, Buffy finally realizes the path she was blindly speeding down.

In the follow-up episode, faith tries to cover up the killing and then, later, tries to blame it on Buffy. Fortunately, Giles sees right through that and everyone turns on Faith. Desperate and alone, she turns to the season's Big Bad, the Mayor, and offers herself as henchwoman.

Faith's turn is comparable to Angel's from the previous season, but it packs a much lesser punch since the emotional investment wasn't as strong. That said, Faith is a tragic character, and her fall to the dark side happened in large part because she felt abandoned by what should have been her surrogate Scooby family. These two episodes only scratch the surface of all that could be said about Faith, but what we get here is solid stuff.

MATTHEW L. MARTIN

#51 – POTENTIAL
SEASON 7, EPISODE 12

Dawn takes some time to grow on you. Some fans never took to her, but while I found her a bit annoying in season 5, I at least appreciated the turmoil the character was going through, especially in the latter half of that year. In season six everyone was a miserable mess, so it's hard to judge her too harshly there.

Season seven is where Dawn finally finds her place in the Scoobies, but that comes after she is teased as someone who could "potentially" be the next slayer. Watching her realization that she is not "special" is heart-wrenching, but then Xander has his shining moment in a beautiful monologue where he makes her (and the audience) appreciate this character for what she is not.

#50 – THE YOKO FACTOR & PRIMEVAL
SEASON 4, EPISODES 20-21

In the first, Spike breaks up the Scoobies (for a sec). In the second, Buffy dispatches of the "Big Bad" of Season 4, the robo-demon Adam (complete with 3.5in Floopy Drive for max cringe). The former is the fun one. The second, despite all the grief the Initiative Arc gets, and rightly so, is a great "season finale-feeling" episode.

BUFFY THE VAMPIRE SLAYER

#49 – BAND CANDY
SEASON 3, EPISODE 6

Buffy's mom has sex with Giles. On the hood of a police car.

Twice.

#48 – ENEMIES
SEASON 3, EPISODE 17

Faith tries to seduce Angel, to turn him into Angelus so he can join Team Mayor. No one seems to get that it's not sex that triggers Angel losing his soul, it's a moment of pure bliss. He's not a eunuch (as he will often remind us on his own show). Faith's attempts backfire spectacularly, but not without her getting some excellent psychological daggers plunged into Buffy's mind in the process.

As said, her turn is not as emotionally charged as the Angelus arc in season two, but Faith offers something else: Faith is what Buffy could have turned into without a stable support system. We should pity Faith, which makes her all the more effective as a villain.

MATTHEW L. MARTIN

#47 –STORYTELLER
SEASON 7, EPISODE 16

Andrew is a bit polarizing in that he's almost entirely a comedic relief character and his brand of comedy can be somewhat grating. Season seven suffered from having so many characters to juggle it was hard for any one of them (outside of the core Scooby gang) to stand out. Andrew was maybe the only one who became a semi-regular in the final season to properly integrate into the group. Well, he didn't "integrate," per se; he was basically a house hostage, but darn it if he didn't have such a "glass half full" perspective on it.

"Storyteller" gives Andrew the podium and lets him walk us through a day in the life of Buffy and her pals. There are some hilarious sight gags and little asides thrown in by the narrator but the real magic of the episode comes in the finale, where Buffy forces Andrew to come to terms with murdering Jonathan. The final shot sees him—the comedic relief—tearfully stating his belief that he would die, and that he deserves to, ending an otherwise fun episode on a heavy and effective note.

#46 – SLEEPER
SEASON 7, EPISODE 8

Spike is being used by the First like a hypnotism victim. He knows it and wants to die for it. One of the consequences of having a soul is having to deal with guilt, and even though we've seen people like Warren (ordinary, souled humans) show their capacity to switch off guilt, the fact is you have to work on being that level of psychopathic. Spike hasn't had a soul in centuries. He's out of practice and his turmoil in this episode is the standout.

#45 – THE REPLACEMENT
SEASON 5, EPISODE 3

In this great comedy episode, Xander gets split in two. It works as an allegory for the season's arc (Glory and Ben, Buffy and Dawn, etc) and provides plenty of rich material for Nicholas Brendon to mine. Watching the "good Xander" be everything the "real Xander" wished he could be is both hilarious and sad, which is also the perfect summary of Xander himself.

#44 – HELP
SEASON 7, EPISODE 4

Cassie Newton seems like a character too well-acted, and too thought-out to be as lightly used as she was. She seems like a regular on a Buffy spinoff show. And since much of season seven feels like the Scoobies are observing a Buffy spinoff show take place around them, I guess that makes sense. Her ability to predict the future is haunting and cleverly handled, especially the tease regarding Spike and Buffy.

Gone too soon, IMO.

#43 – HELLS BELLS
SEASON 6, EPISODE 16

Season six is the year where everyone's worst selves dominated. Xander has always struggled with insecurities, personal fears, and a nagging worry that he will end up a failure. Those dark thoughts come to a head on his wedding day where a visitor claiming to be him from the future shows him the life he's stepping into, one in which he is a deadbeat husband much like his loathsome father.

The idea that Xander would only grow more and more unworthy of Anya leads him to break off the wedding, and even when he learns the truth that the so-called time-traveler was really a demon out for revenge on Anya (a brilliant twist), Xander still runs away, knowing that the demon merely forced him to admit what he had already been stewing over in his subconscious. Of all the season six episodes that make me disappointed for the Scoobies, this one is the hardest to watch. Poor Xander. Poor, poor Anya.

#42 – AFTER LIFE
SEASON 6, EPISODE 3

At this point, we don't yet know the big secret about where Buffy has been between seasons 5 and 6. All we know is she came back rattled and unsure of everything. The show cleverly kept her away from the rest of the gang throughout the first episode, so all that payoff is unleashed on us here.

The Scoobies' euphoria contrasted by Buffy's obvious pain is hard to watch the first time; seeing it after learning the truth makes it even more tragic. By the end of the episode, she confesses to Spike that she was ripped away from Heaven, setting the stage for season six to be Buffy's most emotionally-pained year ever.

MATTHEW L. MARTIN

#41 – INTERVENTION
SEASON 5, EPISODE 18

This is the Vision Quest episode, in which Buffy meets the first slayer, who tells her that Buffy's gift is death. She takes that to mean killing. By the end of the season, she'll have reinterpreted the first slayer's words into something much more beautiful, and heartbreaking.

And Buffy kisses Spike for the first time here.

#40 – SAME TIME SAME PLACE
SEASON 7, EPISODE 3

This episode features the last best use of a "creepy monster of the week" and boy is it a doozy. This thing eats you alive. That's it. That's its thing. But watching it peel away a piece of Willow's belly and munch on it like a piece of soft bacon gives me chills every time. The show's come a long way from the hilariously cheesy praying mantis costume in season one.

The episode's highlight is the way it plays the same scene twice-over, once with Willow (who is otherwise invisible) and then again with the Scoobies (who can't see her). It's an effective bit of editing and makes for a very fun watch.

BUFFY THE VAMPIRE SLAYER

#39 – LIFE SERIAL
SEASON 6, EPISODE 5

Is this episode's high placement a controversial choice? I don't think so. While the trio hardly makes for the best season-long foil, they're not really supposed to be. They're red herrings. The real foils of season six are the Scoobies themselves, and their own worst impulses. Watching Buffy go through a Groundhog Day-like time loop is hardly the most original idea in sci-fi/fantasy storytelling, but the humor derived from it is what carries the day.

#38 – SUPERSTAR
SEASON 4, EPISODE 17

Jonathan is maybe my favorite C-tier character who later upgraded to the B-tier. He's a lovable loser, the kind of kid everyone knew in High School; that guy who no one actually hated, but no one was actually friends with either. He just sort of...existed. Superstar takes that guy and makes him the star of the show, literally; even the opening credits are all Jonathan all the time.

As expected, someone who has never known popularity doesn't know how much is too much, so the world he creates is hilariously over the top. I could quibble with the larger implications and potential consequences of such a spell but who cares. It's a comedy episode, and one of the best in the show's library.

#37 – EARSHOT
SEASON 3, EPISODE 18

Buffy gains the ability to hear everyone's thoughts, including the fact that her mom had sex with Giles. On the hood of a police car.

Twice.

As with many other comedy-heavy episodes, like "Storyteller" and "I Was Made to Love You," this one ends with Buffy overhearing someone seemingly planning a school shooting. She intercepts...Jonathan, but he's not about to kill anyone else, only himself.

The episode was delayed until a few weeks before the start of season four due to the timing of it: The infamous Columbine School Shooting happened right as the episode aired. As for Buffy overhearing someone plotting to kill students, that was Lunch Lady Dorris (or whatever her name is) with a hilariously cartoonish box of rat poison.

So yeah, considering the real-life circumstances, I can see them not wanting to air something with such a light-hearted punchline.

BUFFY THE VAMPIRE SLAYER

#36 – I ONLY HAVE EYES FOR YOU
SEASON 2, EPISODE 19

Your opinion of this episode will largely depend on if you appreciate subtext and allegory in your storytelling. If you prefer things to be laid out straight and plain, then this will probably seem like a goofy, high school drama-looking one-off without much purpose.

Under the surface, however, is a beautiful allegory of the doomed romance between Buffy and Angel (currently Angelus). That it uses ghosts and body possession to tell that allegory is just a product of the genre. I was fine with it, especially since I happen to love the climactic (purposefully overly dramatized) scene between Buffy and Angelus.

#35 – AMENDS
SEASON 3, EPISODE 10

Angelus is arguably the best Big Bad Buffy ever tangled with. He was nasty, cruel, remorseless, and capable of shocking acts of violence and evil, all with a cackle and a smile. The fact that he was also Buffy's lover, given over to the dark side as it were, only added to the drama. Season two ended with the sublime

"Becoming 1-2," at the end of which, Buffy ran her ex-lover through the heart with a sword.

This show just loves its visual metaphors.

Angel was too good a character to keep away, however, so it was hardly a shock when he returned in season three. How to re-integrate him back into the fold was something the season spent half a year dealing with. The climax of that is this episode, one which—as the title implies—offers Angel the chance to make amends for the wrongs he did.

We get our first "look" at the final Big Bad in the series, the infamous "First Evil" but it's Angel's own inner turmoil that's the real villain of the episode. He's prepared to let the sun rise on him and kill him, despite Buffy saying he can make amends and do right again. Fate agreed with her, it seems, as southern California had a sudden and near-miraculous White Christmas; snow fell on Sunnydale, blocking the sun and keeping Angel alive, to rededicate himself to "the fight."

It's a beautiful episode, directed by Joss Whedon, and while it might not be as impactful as many of his other episodes, it's too beautiful to place any lower.

BUFFY THE VAMPIRE SLAYER

#34 – LIVING CONDITIONS
SEASON 4, EPISODE 2

I'm allowed one episode that is way too high on the list but which I cannot put any lower simply because of how much I love it. I refuse to believe "Living Conditions" is so bad it has to be called a "guilty pleasure." Nonsense; this is arguably my favorite comedic episode of the series. Buffy's new college roommate is a Cher-loving, sweater stealing, milk-labeling roommate from hell.

So of course she's an actual demon.

The best parts of the episode feature Buffy trying desperately to convince the Scoobies to help her kill this seemingly normal woman just because Buffy is convinced she's a hellspawn.

"She irons her jeans! She's evil!"

It doesn't really matter how the story resolves itself. I don't care. It's fine but it's hardly what matters here. What matters is how much fun I have watching it every time I rewatch the series. I get giddy with anticipation as I start season 4, knowing that my low-key favorite "unimportant" episode is coming up.

Chapter Sixteen

EVERY BUFFY RANKED 10/10

Finally we come to the best of the best. These are the greatest episodes of the show. There is only one episode better than this bunch of masterpieces, and the final chapter will be devoted entirely to singing its praises. In the meantime are the thirty-odd episodes that I consider perfect. Are they "flawless"? No. I don't consider perfect and flawless to be synonymous terms when reviewing a piece of art. If I call something perfect it means whatever flaws it does have are not enough to detract in any way from how much I love it. These episodes are...

BUFFY THE VAMPIRE SLAYER

THE PERFECT TENS

#33 – PANGS – SEASON 4, EPISODE 8

The episode is a hair controversial today in the way it portrays Native Americans in a very stereotypical way. I just view it in the same realm as comic book stories from the 50s or sitcoms from the 90s.

There are going to be things that you can get up in arms about if you want. I'm not going to stop you. I'm just going to be sitting here loving every second of Buffy's desperate need for a proper Thanksgiving dinner, the many arrows sticking out of Spike's body (all of them narrowly missing his heart), and the final shot of the episode, when the big secret everyone but Buffy knew (Angel was in town and didn't say hi) is finally revealed, is one of the best "last shots" of any episode in the Buffyverse. Spike's face here is delightful. Everyone's face is delightful.

#32 – LIES MY PARENTS TOLD – SEASON 7, EPISODE 17

Other than the finale, this is the last truly great episode of Buffy. It gives us a killer flashback to Spike as a bad guy, offing a Slayer on a New York metro. It gives us Giles manipulating Buffy to keep her distracted while Wood attempts to kill Spike (the Slayer he offed was his mom; small world). And it gives us a powerful moment of growing up, where Buffy finally tells Giles she's no longer his student, essentially firing him as her Watcher.

We've seen the Buffy/Giles relationship grow strained over the years, especially post-resurrection, and while it's heartbreaking to see it break down this way, it makes sense: This isn't the first time Giles has broken her trust under the guise of "Watcher knows best." But this is the first time Buffy has realized she's old enough and mature enough now to walk away.

#31 – TABULA RASA
SEASON 6, EPISODE 8

After seven episodes of season six, it's easy to feel beaten down by all the sadness, angst, and drama swirling around it. Even the episode just before this, while it's a fun showboat of a time, it packs more pathos and heartbreak in its runtime than some entire seasons of Buffy.

This episode serves as a nice respite. Everyone loses their memory, which means they forget while they're all so miserable all the time, and what follows is a game of misplaced identity.

BUFFY THE VAMPIRE SLAYER

The result is the lightest, easiest, breeziest episode of the season, and a fun reminder of simpler times before the darkness takes over once more.

#30 – SELFLESS
SEASON 7, EPISODE 5

Final seasons often feel like final seasons because they often pause to focus on a character who might otherwise not get an entire episode devoted to them. Anya is the star here, and after instantly fitting into the show as a series regular, she reminds us all that she used to be a villain and still has the skill to be bad.

The best part about "Selfless" is either Buffy's immediate readiness to chop off Anya's head once she learns about the murder at the Frat House, or its the fact that Buffy succeeds in driving the weapon into Anya's chest, giving us a half-second to think "holy crap she just murked her!" before we're reminded that, no, demons aren't dispatched so easily.

MATTHEW L. MARTIN

#29 – FOREVER
SEASON 5, EPISODE 17

An episode as monumental as "The Body" needs proper follow-up. Rightly does the show focus on Dawn, the least acquitted with death among the group. What follows is a series of terrible decisions, both done by her and by Buffy, that make you say "no don't!" and "I totally get it" all at once. It's not quite the heart-destroyer that the episode just before it was (none are), but it's gut-wrenching in its own right, and a powerful outing.

#28 – CONVERSATIONS
WITH DEAD PEOPLE
SEASON 7, EPISODE 7

Four stories, Four dead people, Four conversations, each one written by a different member of the staff, with the Buffy story being written and directed by Joss himself. No surprise, it's the snappiest and most introspective of the quartet, but the other three pack plenty of dramatic punch as well.

The only missing player is Xander, which is fine. This is an unusual episode, not just because of the structure of the plot, but in the way it is presented. There's an odd title card at the start (something that happens nowhere else in the show, other than the intentionally set-apart "Once More With Feeling"), and a kind of dreamlike quality to it all.

None of the heroes interact with each other, making it feel like a series of short stories rather than an episode of TV. At times you might even wonder if the characters are under collective hypnosis. The end result is an episode—maybe the last one in the show—that sticks with you and makes you want to rewatch it immediately upon completion.

#27 – SCHOOL HARD
SEASON 2, EPISODE 3

Enter Spike. In a lot of ways, this is the true beginning of season two. The first episode served more as closure to the season one finale, and the second felt more like a holdover script from the cheesier days of the first season. Here, Spike and Drusilla come to town, crash the Parent/Teacher Conference, and begin their time as "usually the most interesting people on screen whenever they're on-screen" in both this show and in Angel to come.

Spike is the character the show never knew it needed till it had him, never realized how important he was until he was MIA in season three, and would never be taken for granted again once he was back for good in season four. Drusilla is simply magnetic. She's maybe the most underrated character in the Buffyverse.

#26 – FEAR ITSELF
SEASON 4, EPISODE 4

Buffy's Halloween episodes—three in all—are all a treat. This one features the Scoobies caught in the most "Scooby" environment possible: A Haunted House. Of course, this being Buffy, and with Buffy being in college, it's a Haunted "Frat" House, but the hijinks are all there, and the gags are abundant.

Anya's fear of bunnies is mined to perfection. Giles showing up with a chainsaw to cut his way into the house is wonderful. And the final scene, where the demon behind all the horror is finally revealed...to be an action-figure-sized non-threat, is the ultimate punchline to an episode that serves no grand purpose other than to be entertaining.

BUFFY THE VAMPIRE SLAYER

#25 – REVELATIONS
SEASON 3, EPISODE 7

Maybe my favorite thing about Revelations is that, while I saw the twist coming a mile away, I was still engrossed in the way it played out. You never quite know how Joss and co. are going to play with your expectations, and in this case, the reveal that Gwendoline Post was the baddie all along was hardly a shock. The manner in which she was dispatched...now that was a shock.

Get it? Get it?

Yeah you get it.

#24 – LOVERS WALK
SEASON 3, EPISODE 8

The fact that Xander could score with someone as stunningly gorgeous as Cordelia is enough to strain credulity, especially when you consider how Joss Whedon viewed the character as a proxy version of himself. That said, when you consider that Xander had a great thing going but then blew it on a side-relationship with Willow, suddenly it all starts to make sense: Xander is exactly the kind of person who would fall backward into an amazing thing and then ruin it by not using his head.

Lovers Walk ends the Xander/Cordy romance, one which I loved for every minute of its existence. It also ends the Willow/Xander secret love, one which I found delightfully well-written, but did not enjoy as a lover of the characters. The episode's great, too.

#23 – SEEING RED
SEASON 6, EPISODE 19

This is a hard episode to watch. Spike's attempted rape happens here. Warren attempting to murder Buffy happens here. Tara dying in the most senseless and fluky way happens here. The latter was a bold choice, and it was really the best way to handle something as unexpected as a gun.

Honestly, the moment Warren whipped out a literal handgun, I remember gasping. Buffy was a show with demon portals, with swords, with witches casting spells. It was not a show where someone pointed a gun and pulled the trigger. Making Tara's death not be a noble sacrifice or the act of a villain purposefully trying to make the hero suffer, but instead having her be the victim of stray fire is a masterstroke. It doesn't make it (or anything that preceded it) any more "enjoyable" to watch, however.

BUFFY THE VAMPIRE SLAYER

#22 – HALLOWEEN
SEASON 2, EPISODE 6

Buffy's first Halloween episode is the most iconic of the three, and even though it has the silliest plot (put on a costume from the evil costume shop, and you are tricked into thinking you actually are that character), the premise is milked for every ounce of comedic worth. This is still the era of Spike being presented as a credible threat, so the climax, featuring the first proper Buffy/Spike brawl since the villain's debut, is a real treat.

The highlight, however, comes from the way the core trio is affected by the black magic at the heart of the episode: Buffy goes from the genre-twisting hero to the genre-cliched damsel in distress. Xander goes from bumbling damsel in distress to slick, in charge hero. Willow goes from the shyest and most insecure of the bunch, to someone free to be confident and outgoing (catching Oz's eye as a result). The whole episode hangs a lampshade on the development of the Scoobies, and has a ton of fun in the process, too.

MATTHEW L. MARTIN

#21 – TWO TO GO & THE GRAVE
SEASON 6, EPISODES 21-22

Dark Willow was probably not the villain anyone predicted when season six started. That's because, as has been said already, the true Big Bad of this year is the collective worst impulses of the Scoobies themselves. Buffy, Xander, and Willow are their own worst enemies.

Xander wrestles with his own feelings of inadequacy. He loses the fight on the day of his wedding.

Willow wrestles with controlling her lust for power. She loses the fight when she crashes the car with Dawn. Buffy wrestles with depression after being pulled out of Heaven and brought back to this miserable planet.

Unlike the others, Buffy doesn't hit a rock-bottom point midway through the season. Her lowest point comes here, at the end of the season, when she finds herself in a literal grave (right where she started the year).

Meanwhile, Dark Willow is ready to blow up the earth as a way to escape the pain of losing Tara. Who saves the day? It's not Buffy; it's the Zeppo. It's the failure. It's the inadequate one. It's the only one who could talk Willow off the ledge. Xander saves the world this time in a beautiful, tear-inducing scene.

BUFFY THE VAMPIRE SLAYER

As the sun shines on a saved world, Buffy crawls out of the grave...again. Unlike at the start of the season, she does so this time with a renewed sense of hope. People can hate on season six all they want, but credit to Joss and co. for sticking with the theme of the year and bringing the arc to a fantastic moment of closure.

#20 – A NEW MAN
SEASON 4, EPISODE 12

Also known as the one where Giles turns into a giant monster that only Spike can understand, leading to a buddy-cop episode that I can probably watch fifteen times in a row and never not adore. The greatest moment comes when Giles—ever the prim and proper gentleman—asks Spike to pull over so he can get out of the car and harass the annoying Mrs. Initiative lady. From beginning to end, this episode is wonderful.

#19 –THE WISH
SEASON 3, EPISODE 9

Season three is such a relentlessly great season, it's hard to pick one episode here and there and elevate them above the rest. It struck the perfect balance of episodic and serialized that the other six seasons never quite hit. Others had killer stand-alone outings (season four) or a great arc (season two), but none melded the two into one quite like the third year.

"The Wish" follows the events of Lovers Walk, which ended with the breakup of Xander and Cordelia. Blaming all her recent misery on Buffy (because of course), Cordy makes a wish to a vengeance demon named Anya, wishing for a reality where Buffy never came to Sunnydale.

The result is the "Yesterday's Enterprise" of the show: An utter dystopia alternate reality where vamps rule the streets, fear grips the hearts of all, and life is a living nightmare. In the midst of this, there is humor to the nines. Everyone gets a chance to play their "mirror universe" selves, none better than Willow, whose turn as a vampire was so well-received, it led to a sequel episode later in the season...

#18 –DOPPELGANGLAND
SEASON 3, EPISODE 16

Really, I don't rate this episode higher or lower than "The Wish," but since they don't occur in succession, I couldn't combine them. They are spiritual siblings, though, and both hit the same comedic notes to great effect. The twist here is the Vamp-Willow from Cordy's alternate reality switches places with good Willow, leading to our sweet and chipper heroine having to act evil. The results are pretty much perfect.

#17 – FOOL FOR LOVE
SEASON 5, EPISODE 7

Foreshadowing, set-up, subtext: You name it, this episode has it in spades. This is the one where Spike talks about the previous Slayers he killed and when he, in the heat of the moment, makes a pass at Buffy (having recently realized he had a crush on her). She rejects him in the most brutal of ways, harkening back to the pathetic love-sick loser man he once was before he was bitten and turned.

This episode is the companion to Angel's "Darla" episode, which aired the same night on the WB. Watching them concurrently features plenty of crossover moments and tells a complete story of the origin and early years of the Buffyverse's resident Vampire quartet. Together they're one of the best two-parters (of a sort) Joss and co. ever did.

MATTHEW L. MARTIN

#16 – THIS YEAR'S GIRL
& WHO ARE YOU
SEASON 4, EPISODES 15-16

Here is a simple premise, done in different ways on different shows of similar genre. It's the only Freaky Friday gag, only not between parent and child, but peers or, in this case, enemies. Faith and Buffy switch bodies, leading to some great acting from Sarah Michelle Gellar (pretending to be Faith in Buffy's body) and Eliza Dushku (pretending to be Buffy in Faith's body).

The climactic fight, when Faith (in Buffy's body) begins pummeling her real face, screaming about how worthless she is and how much she hates her, is an especially dramatic moment, executed flawlessly. Faith was never a character I could completely hate, unlike Angelus. It's too easy to pity her, and this two-parter reminds us why.

#15 – ANGEL
SEASON 1, EPISODE 7

While "Prophesy Girl" was the first episode that really felt like it got Buffy, "Angel" is the first one to show that the series was more than just an episodic "monster of the week"

259

series. The mysterious hunk from the opening episode finally has a bit of his past unearthed, taking him from mild curiosity to instant person of interest.

Angel's backstory, being a demon cursed with a soul and thus forced to endure the guilt of—and work to atone—his past misdeeds, makes for a wonderful arc, one which only begins here and doesn't reach its apex until the character's own final episode in his own spinoff show.

#14 – PASSION
SEASON 2, EPISODE 17

This was the first non-event episode that blew me away. By that, I mean I'm supposed to see something like "Surprise/Innocence" as an episode where they pull out all the stops. This, on the other hand, is just a random episode in the second half of season 2. And really, were it not for this one, a lot of the post-Angelus heel turn would have been kind of a bummer.

The two-parter to kick off the arc is incredible. The two-parter to end it is incredible. And in between is a lot of typical, run-of-the-mill, Buffy shenanigans episodes. The only difference is Angelus sometimes pops up in a threatening way. The exception to all that is "Passion," which gets us into the psyche of Angelus, helping us understand why he likes to toy with his victims before finally devouring them.

Along the way, viewers are treated to a heartwarming subplot focusing on the relationship between Giles and Jenny which, for everyone who knows how this show goes, can only spell disaster. Sure enough, by the end of the episode, Jenny—who had been working on a way to bring Angel back—is killed by Angelus, and we're left to pick up the pieces.

Easily the best thing about the episode is that you simultaneously hate Angelus for killing Jenny, and also pity him because—deep down inside—is the good person Angel who has been deprived (we think) of the way to be restored. Giles' reaction to Jenny's death is an all-timer, as is his sobbing with Buffy soon after. One of the finest "normal" episodes of the show, easily.

#13 – SOMETHING BLUE
SEASON 4, EPISODE 9

Willow accidentally casts a spell that causes, among other things, Giles to go blind, Xander to become a literal "demon magnet," and Buffy/Spike to fall in love.

Unbridled hilarity ensues.

#12 – CHOSEN
SEASON 7, EPISODE 22

For a show that had so many great finales (five of the seven are in the top ten), it's interesting that the last one ever—the finale of the whole enchilada—missed out on cracking the top-ten. There's nothing particularly wrong with "Chosen." It's the 12th best episode, in my opinion, but as a finale, it felt a bit too connected to the several serialized episodes building up to it.

There wasn't as much of a stand-alone plot as other end-of-year blowoffs had. That's a minor complaint, though, as there are dozen little moments that make me cheer, make me gasp, and make me weep. It might not be the show's best season-ender, but it's one of genre TV's best show-enders, that is for sure.

#11 – THE ZEPPO
SEASON 3, EPISODE 13

I think we can all agree there's no way a character like Cordelia Chase knows who Zeppo Marx is, yes? Setting that aside, an episode that begins with the premise that Xander is dead weight, then follows him around highlighting just how useless he is in one of Buffy's many "end of the world" mega-events is a brilliant premise.

The fact that Xander doesn't swoop in to save the day, either heroically or inadvertently but instead remains the unneeded piece of the puzzle is the cherry on top. From beginning to end, this episode grabs you with its hook and doesn't let go, leaving you thrilled by Xander's B-tier adventure, and laughing hysterically at the little glimpses of the melodrama happening with the rest of the Scoobies.

#10 – THE PROM
SEASON 3, EPISODE 20

If "The Prom" had been the finale of season three, even without resolving the issue with Faith and the Mayor, 1 wouldn't even complain. 1 rank this with Passion as one of the best "normal" episodes of the show. The final scene, which shows Buffy finally getting the recognition she deserves from her peers for saving the day time and again, is one of the finest "feel good" moments in genre TV history.

And for a show that loves to sucker you in with a sweet moment only to stab you in the gut right as you start to sigh, it was a welcome relief for the episode to end on a genuine high note for a change. Buffy deserved every bit of that Class Protector Award.

BUFFY THE VAMPIRE SLAYER

#9 – PROPHESY GIRL
SEASON 1, EPISODE 12

Buffy's first season was a messy one, but throughout its protracted run, there were glimpses of what the show could evolve into. In the final episode, all those pieces came together for the first truly great outing. The buildup to Buffy's confrontation with The Master was not as excitedly handled as it would be with the Big Bads of later years, but the fight itself, featuring Buffy dying(!) before being resurrected and finishing the job, is handled with aplomb.

When the theme song kicks in as she marches to the final fight, there's a feeling that comes over you, realizing that the bud has finally blossomed. It would continue to hone its craft and perfect its formula, but in the first of seven finales, it realized the show it was trying to be.

#8 – RESTLESS
SEASON 4, EPISODE 22

After the disappointment of the Initiative arc, Joss Whedon and co. treated the fans who stuck with it to a finale separate from robo-monsters, government secrets, and pretend soldier boys. Instead, we were given something mysterious, something intangible, something akin to a fantasy TV version of the Book of Revelation. "Restless" is a dream-infused episode, and is—in my opinion—the best representation of what actual dreams are like ever depicted on screen.

This is something out of David Lynch's catalogue, with non-sequiturs, familiar characters in bizarre forms, and familiar places in mind-twisting styles. Prophesies for future episodes are aplenty here, including one foreshadowing the main character's death and another hinting at a character joining the show that no one ever could have predicted.

You can watch "Restless" a dozen times and always come away appreciating something new about it. It might not have been the season finale the writers intended when the year began, but it's easily the most fascinating one they ever produced.

#7 – GRADUATION DAY 1-2 – SEASON 3, EPISODES 21-22

Every season finale of Buffy, with the exception of season six, was designed to function as a "series" finale if the show was never renewed. Had the show ended after a season, I would have found the finale frustrating in that it seemed to finally figure out what it was trying to be right as it was canceled.

Had it ended after season two, I would have been sad because it would have ended right as it was great. Season three, however, had an ending that would have been a perfect send-off if need be.

The ending of the Big Bad's plot is of secondary importance here. Everyone graduates high school. The school blows up. Buffy's class assists her in fighting the monsters that have been terrorizing everyone. All the Scoobies get great moments to shine. Angel rides off into the sunset shadows to start his own show. There's closure everywhere you turn. It's a beautiful ending at the end of a phenomenal season. Thank goodness there was more.

#6 – THE GIFT
SEASON 5, EPISODE 22

Had the show not been picked up by UPN, this would have been Buffy's series finale. Unlike the previous three years, this is a single episode installment, but it wraps up the arc of the season and sends the heroine out in the most beautiful and poignant way imaginable. "The Gift" is all about Buffy's willingness to do anything to save the day, even if that means dying. That's how the first season ended, except Buffy wasn't trying to die on that occasion; she lost a fight. The second ended with her being willing to sacrifice her lover to save the world. This one ends with her sacrificing herself to save the world...something she did "a lot," as her gravestone said.

The final two shots of the episode, which occur quickly to fit them into the allotted runtime, almost happen too fast for the viewer even to process it. Buffy dies, and we see everyone surrounding her body, silently wailing in agony. The camera cuts quickly to her tombstone, lingering over her freshly laid grave, and then fades to black just as rapidly.

The hurried nature of it works to its benefit; everything else to be said was already said in the moments leading up to her sacrifice. This is who she is: She saves the world (a lot), even if it means dying for it. What a hero.

#5 – SURPRISE/INNOCENCE
SEASON 2, EPISODES 13-14

These two episodes form the moment when Buffy went from an okay little show, on a little-watched network, to the show you were missing out on if you weren't watching it. Buffy is a seven-season show that can definitely be divided into two unequal parts: There is the period before "Surprise," and the period after.

There is before Angelus took Buffy's innocence, and after. From here on out, Buffy is not just a show about a girl fighting monsters; it's a show about a woman wrestling with the weight of the world on her shoulders.

#4 – BECOMING 1-2
SEASON 2, EPISODES 21-22

The two-parter "Becoming" combine to be the best finale of the show. Despite, as said, the somewhat average-feeling run of episodes (other than "Passion") leading up to the finale, the stakes and the showdown that was looming were never forgotten. It was clear, especially after "Passion," that the Buffy/Angelus feud would come to a head in the finale of the season.

A first-time viewer would not be thought a fool for thinking it would end with Angelus' death and subsequent removal of David Boreanaz from the series. Indeed, the finale did end with Angelus' death, but what was not expected was the fact that Angel was re-souled in the moments just before Buffy "killed" him.

It would have been easy to play it more conventionally, to have Buffy slay the hero-turned-villain and then mope about it for an episode or two. It would have been even easier and safer for Buffy to save Angel and the two of them team up to defeat someone like Spike. It even would have been easy for Buffy to save Angel after dooming him to the hell dimension or to have Angel be saved and killed without Buffy ever realizing it. Instead, Joss and co. went for maximum drama: Buffy saved Angel and then, because the world was still on the line, killed him.

If Surprise/Innocence is the two-parter where Buffy's "girlhood" was stolen away from her, then "Becoming" is the two-parter where she forcefully claimed her adulthood on her own terms. If Surprise/Innocence is the two-parter where Buffy (the show) turned the page to become something greater than what it started as, then "Becoming" is the two-parter where the show solidified that change and told everyone this show was here to stay.

#3 – THE BODY
SEASON 5, EPISODE 16

I don't know what I can add to my previous comments on "The Body." There isn't another episode like it in the entire series. There's no music score. There's no monster of the week. There's no quips. There's no gags. "The Body" is the episode that rips our characters away from their fantasy playground and reminds them—and us—that they are mortal people living in a world where people sometimes just die. They don't all get eaten by demons. They don't all get sucked into a portal. They don't all get stabbed dramatically in the heart with a stake or a sword. Sometimes people have brain aneurysms, and they just drop dead.

Joyce battled a brain tumor all season long, the ultimate red herring. For the multiple episodes she struggled with the malady, we watched Buffy struggle to hold it together. We watched her at the hospital, bloodshot as she worried over her mom. We watched her at the kitchen sink, crying silently in front of the running water while she tried to do dishes. We watched her gripped with fear as she waited for news of her mother's surgery. And then, when it was all over, we watched relief overtake her. Joyce is fine. Everything is okay. And it was. The problem was resolved.

And then she died anyway.

And it was the needlessness of it, the senselessness of it, the randomness of it, that makes everything about it so beautifully captured on film. It's a death that wouldn't work on a normal dramatic show. On the other hand, this is fantasy; something as mundane as dying of an aneurysm is the most shocking way someone could die. Watching the characters—who had previously witnessed hundreds of "deaths" (of a sort)—try and fail throughout the episode to process what happened was like being a parent forced to watch your child crying and being unable to console them. You feel helpless.

For forty-some-odd minutes, Joss Whedon turned off the fantastical show and gave us a short film on grieving, loss, trauma, and the frustrated feelings of unfairness that come with losing a loved one to death. It's Emmy worth. Under a different format, I'd say it was Oscar-worthy.

#2 – HUSH
SEASON 4, EPISODE 10

The ranking difference between #3 and #2 is so razor-thin it might as well be a tie. These are two distinctly different episodes, so putting "Hush" one notch above "The Body" is purely because, while I appreciate "The Body" more, I enjoy "Hush." I'm not supposed to enjoy "The Body." I admire it, but I also admire "Hush." This is Joss' silent film. This is the episode where the guy everyone said was a one-trick pony ("he can write good dialogue and that's about it") decided to challenge himself to craft a good episode of TV without any talking (once the plot kicks in, at least).

I don't know if there is a "best thing" about an episode that is flawless from top to bottom, but at least the thing I love the most about it is that the episode is not just content with being a "special attraction." This isn't just an episode you can throw on and admire for its technical achievement while enjoying a story detached from the rest of the narrative. No, the happenings of this episode are integral to the arc of season four.

This is the episode that plants a dozen seeds for the future (Willow and Tara meet here) and reveals major plot points (namely Buffy and Riley discovering each other's secrets). All the while, the backdrop is the show's best-looking and acting villains by a mile. They're just so darn polite as they cut you open and eat your insides!

What makes "The Gentlemen" such amazing one-off villains? Is it the fact that they're silent? Is it their giant, frozen smiles? For me, it's the way they glide along the ground, moving from point-A to point-B with only their gently swaying arms or gently bobbing heads to hint at life.

Once everyone in town is voice-deprived, the real fun of the episode kicks in. Whedon uses every trick, every possible gag, every innuendo, everything he can employ to get every bit of creativity from the premise. This could have been a ninety-minute special feature, but instead, it's a forty-minute, rapid-paced, horror short. It's probably the scariest episode of the so-called "horror fantasy" series, but it knows how to intersperse the thrills and chills with plenty of gags and laughs, too.

You might rank this one below "The Body" but, as I say, they're both 10/10 to me. You might even rank it #1, or you might put "The Body" at the top spot. Wherever you slot it, the odds are good it is placed around the very very top of the charts for Buffy episodes, and with good reason. While "The Body" proved Joss Whedon didn't need jokes to tell a great story, "Hush" proved he didn't even need dialogue.

There's only one episode left and it's the greatest hour of television Joss Whedon ever produced...

Chapter Seventeen

BUFFY'S GREATEST EPISODE

Calling this the "greatest" episode needs some explaining. After all, someone else might very easily place "The Body" at the top of their list, and bump this one to the #2 or #3 spot. Another fan might be inclined to favor something a bit more traditional than either episode, and place something like "Hush" or "The Zeppo" or "Graduation Day 1-2" at the top of their ranking. I suppose you could make a pretty good argument for any of the top dozen or so to be the show's greatest episode and I wouldn't take up stones against you.

For me, I don't use the term "greatest" to mean "most flawless" or even, necessarily, the "best all around." I use "greatest" to mean "the episode most transcendent, or most memorable; the boldest, most souped-up, special-feeling outing in the series." In Marvel terms, I consider Endgame to be the "greatest" MCU movie, even if I also think Infinity War is a "better" film. The epic-ness and hugeness of Endgame places it on a higher tier in my estimation.

And that's how I feel about "Once More With Feeling." You can hold up literally any other "great" or "awesome" or "excellent" or any other adjective-episode and, other than maybe "The Body," they all feel like Buffy episodes, only done very very well.

Sure, in "Hush," everyone loses their voice and 75% of the episode is played out like a silent movie. It's a remarkably well-done gimmick but, at the end of the day, it's still just a Buffy episode, only with a layer of cleverness on top.

"The Body," is the most un-Buffy like episode of them all, even more un-Buffy like than this one. Other than the final scene, which features an apparently obligatory vampire slaying in the morgue, there's nothing really to link it to the themes or plots of the show around it. The quips are gone. The music is absent. There's no talk of the Big Bad. There's no quest to go on in the vain hopes of undoing what has happened. In

"The Body," Buffy the Vampire Slayer stops being itself for an hour so that its characters can process the cold and bitter reality of mortality. It's because of that stark un-Buffyness, despite how utterly masterful it is as a piece of fiction, I could only slot it as #3. "Hush" got the nod over it simply because it was a bit more "Buffy-like."

"Once More With Feeling," being a musical, is naturally going to be viewed as the most unusual episode of the show. But really, it's more traditional than either "Hush" or "The Body." That being said, had it been an episode content to settle for being a gimmick, with nothing else under the surface, it would not have been rated at the top of the list. There's something else going on here that earns its high praise.

So let me sing its praises in a few different ways, and hopefully settle on what it is that makes it "the greatest." To begin with, here's something I said in the season six write-up...

What's most remarkable about this year is how the episode everyone loves from the season, "Once More With Feeling," is often lauded as being a happy oasis in a sea of gloominess. In reality, "Once More With Feeling" is the most poignant episode of the whole series.

It might not be as straightforwardly sad as "The Body" but it's a close second. The difference is that it hides its sadness behind the song and dance numbers. When you read the lyrics to the songs in question you soon realize that Joss used his "musical episode" as a way to sort of lay out his thesis for the whole season.

What sets this episode apart from basically every other "musical episode" that has been done as a copycat of this one, is that the songs are not sung just for the sake of singing. Yes, there's the Mustard Song, and the Parking Ticket Song, which are quick little gags and nothing more, but when you look at the big numbers starring the main cast, they're not just singing pointless lyrics. They're expressing the thoughts they've been wrestling with for some time and, for one reason or another, had been unwilling to share out loud.

The villain of the picture, the demon Sweet, is the most successful fiend in the history of the show. He wins in basically every possible way short of getting Buffy to die, which was only ever a secondary goal for him anyway. His job is to sow mischief, discord, and unease amongst the Scoobies. His job is to take the gently smoldering fires of their collective depression, anxiety, and other negative emotions, and turn up the heat until the gang is a raging fire of discontentment.

Everything that happens in this episode could have happened in a dozen different ways. The Scoobies could have come under the influence of a Demon who can read minds. They could have broken a magical lamp at the Magic Shop that makes them all share minds for a day. They could have had a Bottle Episode in Buffy's house in the middle of a heatwave, when the air conditioning breaks, and they're all hot and frustrated and on each other's nerves till they unload all their frustrations out for everyone to hear.

There are countless ways to reveal the dark secrets of the group, or even to hint at problems that will come to a head later in the season. Joss chose to use music. It was "an excuse" to have a "music episode" but unlike other shows, the music served the story, not the other way around.

Maybe what I love most about the episode is how well it works on multiple levels. In particular, consider the climax: Dawn has been kidnapped by Sweet's minions and Giles sends Buffy off to rescue her. This is standard operating procedure except for the fact that, this time, Giles insists she go alone.

From Giles' perspective, Buffy has become too dependent on others to fight her battles. He especially senses her dependence on him and since he is planning on returning to England (which Buffy does not know), he needs her to grow up and stand more solidly on her own two feet.

What Giles doesn't seem to grasp is that Buffy is depressed. And why would he grasp that? He doesn't yet know that they pulled her out of Heaven at the beginning of the season. He's harboring his secrets. Buffy is harboring hers.

Later, Giles has a change of heart and rounds up the Scoobies to go aid Buffy (set to the song Walk Through the Fire, one of the most goosebump-inducing sequences in the series). The best part, however, has nothing to do with the Scoobies, because it's not the Scoobies that actually help Buffy.

It's Spike.

Had no one gone to help Buffy, she would have gone alone, and what was her plan? She told the demon Sweet to exchange her life for Dawn's. She was willing to go to Hell (or whatever demon dimension Sweet was from) and, in fact, seemed almost eager to get her life over with. She just wants to feel something, anything, again, even if the feeling is torturous.

Thus, even when the Scoobies arrive, Buffy does her big Something to Sing About number (which, holy cow those lyrics are heartbreaking) and finally confesses that they pulled her out of Heaven (Willow's reaction to the song is devastating; there's so much emotion in that one reaction shot I can't even describe it). Once the truth is out, Buffy starts dancing.

She starts dancing and smoking, knowing it will kill her (as per Sweet's cursed magic). She wants to die, in other words. She wants to get this life over with...and no one can stop her.

Until Spike does.

During the Walk through the Fire montage, Spike is shown separated from the Scoobies. He's not led by Giles out of the Magic Shop. He goes on his own. He decides to help Buffy on his own, in other words. It is he who stops her from dancing, while the others stare in stunned silence at the scene. It is he who tells her the only way to help herself is to keep on living, because ending your life doesn't solve anything.

In my opinion, this scene is one of the most beautiful expressions of suicide prevention ever depicted on TV.

And even though the episode ends with Buffy singing to Spike that she just wants to feel and that their kiss isn't real (while Spike, the fool in love he is, just sings that her kiss can make him feel), the point is she chooses Spike over death, and while that's morbid and sad in its own way (and has its own consequences as the season progresses), it's still preferable to her ending her own life.

Spike gives Buffy a stay of execution, in a sense. He gives her a chance to crawl out of her depression. It's something he could offer her that Giles and the rest of the gang could not. It's a beautiful, poignant ending to a beautiful and poignant episode, and, in large part, is the reason I cannot but place it at the top of the list.

Buffy's confession is only one of several hints into the inner thoughts of the heroes. Some of these thoughts are shared between them, forced out through involuntary melody, and sometimes they are sung in private, for only the audience to discover. In both cases, the songs serve to plant the seeds that Joss and co. will water as this dark and depression-fueled season continues.

My ranking of the big songs (not counting the reprises, codas, or fragments that are peppered throughout the episode) from bottom to best:

9) Going through the Motions

The opening number is at the bottom of the list, but not because the song is no good. On the contrary, it does exactly what it needs to do. It wasn't meant to be the biggest number in the episode, but it did have the important task of selling the "idea" of the episode to the viewer tuning in for the first time based on the hype (UPN did give this episode a ton of promotion), or to the Buffy viewer skeptical of the "need" for such an episode.

Making the tune a classic Disney Princess "I want" song was a masterstroke. It sets not only the tone for the episode with its overly theatrical camera work and acting, mixed with classic Buffy humor (like the goat demon's "ow" and the Handsome Damsel she rescues trying, and immediately failing, to woo her), but also underscores the season-long plot of Buffy wrestling with her post-resurrection depression.

It's a simple song but perfectly done, and since this is at the bottom of the list, I'd say that adds up to an overall episode that is (in my opinion) the best in hour of the show's history.

8) What You Feel

Dawn's falsetto isn't the best, but her dancing more than makes up for it. Sweet's raspy jazz-infused voice is a treat, and the tune is so much fun you almost fail to notice just how much exposition you're being fed.

I also can't get over two particular bits of really excellent special effects (for the day and the show's budget): The door that drops revealing a combusted victim and Sweet changing from red to blue. The latter effect is so seamless I marvel every time I see it. I'm sure it was done with a simple trick, but it looks so perfect I always gasp.

7) Under Your Spell

I'm sure this is rated a lot higher on other lists and I get it: It's a beautiful song, beautifully song by Amber Benson's angelic voice, and I like the Disney princess charm effects sprinkled throughout.

The final verse is sultry in a way contrary to how most sexual jokes on Buffy go (they're usually just Xander making the kind of "horny kid in school" jokes that Joss himself probably made all through his teenage years). It's good stuff all around, it just doesn't affect me the way the ones above it do.

6) Rest in Peace

Probably my favorite from a direction standpoint, as Joss shoots it like a late-90s/early 00's music video, with dutch angles, sweeping camera movements, multiple locations, etc. The song's fun too, and as great as Spike is throughout it, my favorite thing to do while it's playing is watch Buffy move silently through the spectacle, acting only with her eyes. It's great stuff.

5) Standing

Anthony Head's ability to sing is probably the reason we have this episode in the first place. The fact that his talent was used to great effect in past episodes allowed Joss to do more and more with music until he finally got to make his musical. Standing might be rated lower on some lists by those who find the song a bit too subdued.

That's the thing, though: These aren't just "songs inspired by Buffy." These are songs sung by Buffy characters to Buffy characters. The songs don't just **service** the plot; they **are** the plot. Between this episode and Giles singing the Exposition Song in Restless, I can't help but think there's an alternate universe out there where Buffy's entire show is a musical that does its exposition and big dialogue reveals through singing.

I want to see that series.

4) I'll Never Tell

Endlessly charming, funny, and sweet. Xander and Anya's duet is a great throwback to the Fred Astaire days of musicals. I love Anya's face when she says "his eyes are beady."

Every line in the song makes me smile, right down to Xander's: "You're the cutest of the Scoobies, with your lips as red as rubies, and your firm yet supple—tight embrace!" It's impossible to listen to this song and not bob your head and grin like an idiot.

Of course, the fact that the song—catchy and seemingly chipper as it is—is really a just way for the two of them to express their premarital insecurities, worries, and deepest, darkest fears (all of which come to a head in the most heartbreaking of ways later in the year, in the episode "Hell's Bells") is another reason why this episode is the greatest.

MATTHEW L. MARTIN

3) I've Got a Theory / Bunnies

I know, most people dismiss this one as a one-joke song, but just hear me out. First, this is the second most fun song, after I'll Never Tell. Second, it's a good showcase for the whole Scooby Gang as even Willow is allowed a line or two.

Obviously, Anya's Bunnies interlude is the highlight everyone thinks of, and yes it's hilariously delightful, but I'm drawn more to the subtler moments, like when Buffy first starts singing and it causes Giles to stop and turn to face her.

Giles' storyline in the episode is about how much he feels Buffy is slipping away from her responsibilities and relying too much on him for the heavy lifting. So when she sings "I've got a theory; it doesn't matter..." he can't help but turn and focus on his champion, to see how she's handling this.

While everyone else is singing harmony with Buffy, Giles is quiet—I think as an expression of his desire to leave the group and force them to mature without him—until, near the end of the verse, Buffy looks right at him and smiles as she sings, which makes Giles smile and start singing, a sign that he loves her too much to walk away from her (yet).

Near the end, they all sing the line "we'll pay the price; it's do or die," after which Buffy shrugs and solos "hey I've died twice." When she does, Joss cuts right back to Giles, who laughs at the line, completely taken in by her charm. He can't leave this girl; he lost her and just got her back.

Little does Giles know, Buffy's quip about dying was really a coping mechanism to hide the genuine depression she feels after being resurrected, a fact which will come to a head at the end of the episode. There's so much poignancy and beauty packed into what we mostly just think of as "Anya's funny bunnies song."

2) Walk Through the Fire

When critics try to dismiss "Once More With Feeling" as a **mere** musical, or when they try to argue that the end result failed to reach the high goal it set for itself, I always shake my head and think of this number, which managed not only to be a rousing song, but which also conveyed a sense of tension and anticipation as the heroes headed for the final showdown.

Joss was already a master at crafting scenes (or sometimes whole episodes) that conveyed a sense of tension and buildup to the big showdown with the baddie; here he pulled off those same feelings Buffy fans were more than accustomed to, only this time through the medium of a sweeping musical number.

That's amazing.

1) Give Me Something to Sing About

The big finish, essentially. It hits every note (no pun intended). It's beautifully sung, powerfully written, and features a ton of great moments. I love Giles saying Buffy needs backup and then sends Tara and Anya to be literal "backup dancers." I love the haunting B-minor to B-diminished when Buffy sings "heaven," and then when Spike sings "living."

I love when Buffy sings "give me something" to Sweet in the most pitiable and pleading way and he just, very subtly, shakes his head 'no.' It's at that point that Buffy realizes she'd rather dance and burn just to feel anything, leading to Spike saving her life. I love, as Buffy is contemplating Spike's advice that she has to go on living, Dawn calls us back to the end of season five, to the moment before Buffy sacrificed herself...

"The hardest thing in the world
is to live in it."

I love the inherent cheesiness that comes with the territory of a musical production, and how the show knew it would never work if it didn't go 100% sincere with it.

The ending is the best example of that, as the heroes all clasp hands and then dramatically separate, foreshadowing the hard days ahead for them. It's a show-stopping finish to a masterpiece episode.

Those reasons, and many more, are why "Once More With Feeling" rises above all the rest to be considered the greatest Buffy the Vampire Slayer episode of them all.

MATTHEW L. MARTIN

CONCLUSION

Looking back, there's no disputing the fact that Buffy the Vampire Slayer never became a monster ratings-grabber. It barely attracted new fans during its initial run on television, and the network that aired it frequently teased pulling the plug and ending it.

What it had going for it, on the inside, was a staff of top-notch writers, led by Joss Whedon at the prime of his life, as well as a huge cast of stars and semi-regulars who never failed to rise to the occasion whenever the spotlight shined their way. What it had going for it, on the outside, was a diehard following of fans who, while small compared to those of other TV shows, sung its praises and extolled its greatness during and long after its time on TV was done.

That's it.

That's the end. Seven seasons of Buffy, plus five seasons of Angel. It all began with a show that was little more than a mid-season replacement on a little-watched network. It began as a show at first regarded as nothing more than a spin-off of a movie already largely forgotten by pop culture enthusiasts. It began with a rocky and messy first season, completely produced and brought to air before any feedback could be given, seemingly tossed to the wolves to fill airtime and little else.

And then it thrived.

Its second season showed maturity in the writing, production, acting, tone. Everything had improved, to the point where, midway through the year, the show had entrenched itself into the zeitgeist of genre fandom, never to relent. Better writing followed in season three, bigger risks were taken in season four, the show arguably reached its zenith at the end of its fifth season, just as its main heroine leapt to her sacrificial death. The resurrection that followed was a rocky and messy one, essentially resetting the table on a new network, in an era where so many copycat shows had come along to put their own spin on the formula.

By the time the series ended, its fans said goodbye with a feeling of satisfaction and contentment rarely enjoyed with long-running shows. Usually, by the end, the fanbase is either united behind the desire for more more more, or they are split in half, with many saying the show should have ended long before.

While Buffy had a few who thought season five should have been the end, by the time the actual last episode aired, there were few to be found who weren't happy to have had another two years with the Scooby gang, and fewer still who weren't happy with how the show said goodbye.

Twenty-five years after it began, and nineteen years after it ended, Buffy the Vampire Slayer remains a quintessential piece of fantasy television. Its premise was silly. Its characters were sillier still. But the whole of it was a magical experience, illustrating the often turbulent journey everyone must take from childhood to adulthood, and the many demons (personal and otherwise) we all must contend with along the way.

Buffy reached her endpoint. She saved the world (a lot) and, as the final moments of her final episode drew to a close, all she could do—all she needed to do—was sigh and allow a satisfied smile to cross over her face, the same smile her fans have every time they go back to Sunnydale, to re-watch the Slayer do her thing.

MATTHEW L. MARTIN

BUFFY THE VAMPIRE SLAYER

OTHER BOOKS FROM THE AUTHOR

The KINGDOM OF ARTHUR series...

The Ill-Winds of Fate
The Headwinds of Destiny
The Quest of Sir Lancelot
The Man with Two Faces
The Lady in The Lake
The Death of Arthur

The FARCICAL ZOMBIE Trilogy

"Gza: Geriatric Zombie Apocalypse"

"Titanic Panic"

**"A German Scientist on
Samuel Clemens' Front Porch"**

MISC BOOKS OF ALL SORTS

Shorts,
a collection of short stories and poems

Buried Deep,
a horror story

El Dorado,
a 19th century tale of vengeance and avarice

The Wildest Town in the West,
a western romp

Adventures of Jon Burrows vol. 1-3,
an *anthology of short tales*

MATTHEW L. MARTIN

OTHER BOOKS FROM THE AUTHOR

The DISHONORED Anthology
The Curse of the Demon Prince
The Daughter of Hachiman
The War of the Sakura trilogy
The Song of Redemption
The Last Son of Yumea
The Man Named Sato
The Death of Emperor Bakshi
The Fall of the House of Tadami
The Massacre at Humao-Chi

THE CHUMPTY DUMPTY TRILOGY OF CHILDREN'S TALES
The Beanstalk Tale
The Wishing-Well War
The Impossible Quest

MORE CHILDREN'S BOOKS
One Halloween Evening

One Christmas-Eve Evening

The Great Mouse Escape

The Troll Who Chose to Read

20k Lightyears from Earth

(AND MORE)

Printed in Great Britain
by Amazon